Participation for All

Participation for All:
A Guide to Legislative Debate

Michael K. Middleton

international debate education association

New York - Amsterdam - Brussels

Published by:
The International Debate Education Association
400 West 59th Street
New York, NY 10019

Library of Congress Cataloging-in-Publication Data
Middleton, Michael K.
  Participation for all : a guide to legislative debate / Michael K.
Middleton.
    p. cm.
 Includes bibliographical references and index.
 ISBN 978-1-932716-20-7 (alk. paper)
 1. Parliamentary practice. 2. Debates and debating. I. Title.
 JF515.M57 2007
 060.4'2--dc22
              2006039556

Printed in the USA

 IDEBATE Press

Contents

SECTION 4: CONDUCTING COMPETITIVE CONGRESSES: GUIDELINES FOR COACHES, JUDGES, AND HOSTS

Introduction

Participation for All provides an introduction to legislative debate. In the United States, this format is called student congress. In other places, it may be termed youth parliamentary or legislative assembly. You also may be familiar with the format and procedures this book discusses from participating in other types of debate, such as Model UN.

You probably want to participate in legislative debate because you are interested in issues affecting your local community, your nation, or the world, and want to learn how decisions are made about policies that affect your life. Student congress gives you the opportunity to examine issues in ways that mirror the real world and, thus, encourage both critical thinking and the understanding of such issues.

To participate effectively in student congress, you must understand the format and know the rules that govern these assemblies. *Participation for All* helps you prepare for the congress and describes some of the activities you will engage in during the session. You will learn how a session is organized and how to write resolutions and bills, construct amendments, and organize speeches. You also will learn the basic rules of procedure. For many debaters, these can be particularly daunting, and so, we have devoted a considerable portion of the book to this topic.

Participation for All explains the most important rules of procedure in language that is accessible to the beginner and in a format that provides a quick reference for the experienced competitor or sponsor. It also offers background on the development of these rules and discusses the major concepts underlying them. Finally, it suggests guidelines for implementing the rules once you have become familiar with them.

This text also helps coaches, judges, and tournament hosts who are new to student congress. The first time you attempt to sponsor a congress, you may find preparation and hosting overwhelming. Or you may worry that as a new coach or judge, you are not up to the task. This book will allay your fears and present you with simple guidelines that will make your experience successful and enjoyable.

Participation for All is divided into four sections, each of which focuses on an important aspect of student congress. Section 1 offers background on legislative assemblies: the goals and benefits of student congresses, and the characteristics, advantages, and disadvantages of the legislative model of debate.

Section 2 focuses on the rules of procedure: the principles underlying the rules and the various types of motions used to conduct the business of the assembly. It also guides you through a student congress session, showing you how the rules are used in practice.

The chapters in Section 3 introduce you to the major activities that occur in legislative forums: you learn how to prepare resolutions and amendments, offer speeches, and use committees to refine ideas.

Section 4 speaks to the concerns of sponsors, providing an overview of the processes involved in coaching, judging, and hosting a competitive tournament. With the guidelines, rules, and practices outlined in these chapters and the official rules of any leagues to which you belong, you should have the information necessary to begin hosting competitions in your own classroom, school, or community.

Each chapter concludes with a quick summary of important concepts. Finally, a series of appendixes condenses much of the information found in the book into accessible tables for easy reference.

If you are a novice to student congress, you can use *Participation for All* as an introduction to the format and its rules. If you are a more experienced debater, you can use it as refresher and a quick reference guide. If you are a sponsor, this text will assist you in coaching, give you strategies for managing an event, and help you train judges or develop your own judging abilities. Whatever your background, this text will help you further your ultimate goal of debating issues important to your community and society.

NOTE: *Participation for All* provides a general summary of the rules and practices of legislative debate and explains the activities that you may engage in across a variety of legislative debate formats. These may change depending on the organization sanctioning the student congress, e.g. participants in the United States competing in NFL, CFL, Model UN, or other legislative formats. Therefore, you should consult the sponsor's manuals before participating in a sanctioned event.

Salt Lake City, UT
October 2006

Section 1

Introducing Legislative Debate

Chapter 1
Student Congress: An Introduction

This chapter explores the benefits of legislative debate. It begins by describing the goals of student congress and then presents the features of these forums that speak to the concerns of young people.

STUDENT CONGRESS

Student congresses are assemblies in which young people address the social and civic issues that concern them in sessions that mirror the legislative process in their own communities. As in other debate activities, participants learn about public speaking and public advocacy, but unlike other forensic events, in student congress the participants control the debate, often choosing the topics they want to discuss. Thus, the issues these assemblies address are frequently of high concern to young people in contrast to the topics assigned to debaters in other formats. And unlike other formats, which are adversarial, student congress encourages the development of common understandings and new insights from shared interaction.

Types of Student Congress

There are two types of student congress: the competitive and the non-competitive models. They often focus on the same issues, come to the same solutions, and teach similar advocacy skills; however, the two models have different goals and outcomes. The competitive model, which is especially popular in the United States, is an exercise in debate. It is distinguished by the inclusion of judges, who rank superior speakers based on breadth of knowledge of the issues discussed and expertise in the rules of legislative debate. While the participants debate issues and discuss solutions, they typically do not act on the measures they pass. Instead, they return to their debate societies and work on perfecting their skills for the next competition.

In contrast, non-competitive congresses emphasize cooperation among participants and create opportunities for them to champion the issues they have discussed and solutions they have developed in public discussions. These assemblies often work with governmental and non-governmental organizations to implement their plans. The non-competitive model extends beyond the assembly, enabling young people to participate in their community and see how the decisions they have made can impact their world. Neither model is superior. Organizers choose the model that suits their goals.

Goals of Competitive Student Congresses	Goals of Non-Competitive Student Congresses
Develop and Award Superior Advocacy Skills Participants are judged on their ability to advocate solutions, develop strong arguments, and generate support for their proposals. **Develop and Award Superior Knowledge of Parliamentary Procedure** Participants are evaluated on their expertise in using parliamentary procedure. As a result, members learn how to generate and suggest solutions to problems in the framework used by decision-making bodies in their community.	**Initiate Change** Participants deliberate issues they think important and develop policies that they can advocate in their communities. By including and fostering all perspectives, the assembly develops a consensus that can be a force for real change. **Encourage Collective Action** Young people refine their ideas based on the input of their peers. They develop a sense of community that enables them to speak to the greater society with the strength of a collective voice. *(continues)*

(continued) Goals of Competitive Student Congresses	Goals of Non-Competitive Student Congresses
Promote Cultural Learning Student congresses encourage the sharing of ideas among people from a wide variety of backgrounds. Encountering diversity in this setting gives young people a deeper understanding of their larger community and how the issues they discuss and solutions they propose impact various groups.	**Promote Cultural Learning** Student congresses enable young people from a wide variety of backgrounds to share ideas. Encountering diversity in these assemblies gives students a deeper understanding of their community and how the issues they discuss and solutions they propose impact various groups.

Participation for All is a guide for participants and organizers involved in either model. The information in the following pages provides an introduction to and discussion of the key elements of student congresses. It attempts to offer insights that benefit participants in both models equally. Ultimately, I hope that this text will encourage you to access the full range of benefits offered by both models, and will provide you with the "know-how" to successfully participate in either.

BENEFITS OF STUDENT CONGRESS

Student congress will help change your attitudes about politics. Through participation, you will gain an understanding of the legislative process and of the complexities surrounding contemporary issues. You will learn to respect other viewpoints and appreciate the importance of negotiation and compromise in the democratic process. Participation should encourage you to see yourself as a knowledgeable citizen who can take part in the political dialogue of your society and have an impact on your community.

The legislative debate format enables you to share concerns and arrive at decisions about issues that affect your life. In most forensic events, participants have no voice in the topic they debate, but in student congresses, *you* and your fellow participants choose the topics you think important and then debate them with your peers. You focus on aspects of the topics that most concern you and develop solutions that reflect your understanding of the issues.

Student congress also teaches you the public advocacy skills you need to become a community leader. This forum fosters openness and tolerance as well as acceptance of diversity. You will learn that all members are equal and have the right to express themselves on an issue. At the same time, you will come to understand that legislatures are productive only if members put aside individual differences for the sake of consensus. Whether attempting to pass a piece of legislation in a competitive student congress or drafting a letter to a non-governmental organization in a non-competitive assembly, you and your fellow participants will discover the importance of finding common ground and working toward common goals on issues you consider significant.

Participation in student congresses also helps you understand the decision-making processes in your local and national legislatures. You learn the rules that govern assemblies—and the important principles underlying the rules—so that your legislature appears less remote. And while discovering how these legislative bodies operate, you also come to understand the problems your representatives face in dealing with the important issues of the day.

Student congress also fosters critical thinking and cultural learning. By focusing on contemporary, controversial issues, it offers you the opportunity to engage in problem solving and negotiations to resolve differences of opinion. And, by bringing together students from diverse backgrounds with different perspectives, these assemblies promote cultural learning.

Finally, in student congress you learn by doing. Rather than reading about legislative procedures or issues in a sterile classroom setting, you experience the process and learn in a self-organized and voluntary manner. You control the subject matter and outcomes. Thus, your experiences and learning are closely aligned with your interests and aspirations.

KEY CONCEPTS FROM CHAPTER 1

Student Congress

- The competitive model of student congress is an exercise in debate.
- The non-competitive model enables you to express your ideas and become actively involved in issues you think important.

Benefits of Student Congress

- It teaches a variety of skills necessary for active citizenship, involvement in social issues, and public advocacy.
- It provides a venue where this involvement can be organized and used to effect change.
- It directly involves you in social issues and provides a way to make that participation real and not just symbolic.
- It increases cultural interaction and cultural exchange through the sharing of perspectives on important public issues.

Chapter 2

Creating an Open Forum: Introduction to the Legislative Model

Now that you have learned about the opportunities and benefits that student congress offers, you will learn about the characteristics of these assemblies. As you will see, these characteristics significantly impact the type of debate that occurs. This chapter begins with a brief introduction to the characteristics of a legislative assembly and then explores the advantages and disadvantages of the legislative model.

CHARACTERISTICS OF LEGISLATIVE ASSEMBLIES

A congress, or any other parliamentary assembly, is a deliberative body that enables its members to engage in diverse and far-reaching discussions about issues they think important under conditions that ensure the equal participation of all members. While these assemblies vary, they share several characteristics outlined in *Robert's Rules of Order*, the most commonly adopted parliamentary authority in the United States:[1]

1. They are comprised of a group of people who meet to decide—"in full and free discussion"—actions, values, and beliefs that the body will endorse.[2]

2. The group meets in one chamber, where every member has an equal opportunity to speak.[3]

3. The discussions of the group are governed by formal rules and procedures that ensure deliberation of even the most contentious issues will not bring the assembly to a halt.[4]

4. Members act in accord with their own judgments, not a predetermined position that they must defend.[5]

5. Each member's opinion is of equal value, as measured by a vote.[6]

6. Members who do not support the assembly's decision continue to participate equally in future deliberations.[7]

7. Assemblies may still deliberate and arrive at decisions on issues even if not all members are in attendance.[8]

ADVANTAGES OF THE LEGISLATIVE MODEL

Student congress offers several advantages over other forms of debate and deliberation.

Participants make better decisions. Student congress provides a forum in which participants debate multiple viewpoints and refine ideas to arrive at what members determine is the best decision. In contrast, in traditional forensic events, the number of participants and the positions they take are severely limited: two academic debate teams argue for or against a predetermined proposition, presenting their ideas only during designated speaking times. Likewise, success is defined by one viewpoint prevailing over the other. Thus, traditional debate may not arrive at the best plan or solution to a problem because a small number of participants presents a very limited number of options. In the parliamentary model, participants representing a wide variety of ideas, values, and beliefs are encouraged to work together to determine the best course of action.

Participants choose the issues for discussion. In traditional debate settings, participants debate a topic, often provided by a topic committee comprised of teachers and organizers, that they may or may not think relevant. They have limited voice in selecting the topic and, as a result, often share little personal investment or interest in the debate's outcome. Student congress, on the other hand, allows participants to introduce topics, thus encouraging far-reaching discussions on a broad range of issues that they consider important.

Large numbers can participate. Whereas a traditional debate format limits participants to small teams of two or three that engage in adversarial discussion, a large number of individuals can participate in a congress. Some assemblies may have as many as 200 or more members. Larger numbers can result in greater diversity, which not only contributes to better debate, but also helps participants develop tolerance and appreciation for other perspectives. By interacting with people of various backgrounds, participants begin to understand each other and see what all people have in common.

Student congress allows members to argue for the position of their choice. Because other debate formats assign participants to a side, the competitors are required to debate for or against a specific proposition regardless of their beliefs on the issue. In contrast, in a legislative assembly, every member has the right to address the topic as that individual sees fit.[9] This concept is a basic principle of legislative assemblies. Combined with rules of procedure that create protections for even the smallest minority, the right to speak ensures that all viewpoints are heard in the debate.

Student congress promotes collaborative decision making. Student congress encourages cooperation so that members can make the best decisions for the common good. Unlike team debate, which focuses on the merits of two predetermined positions, student congress relies on a synthesis of ideas that emerge from the speeches and views that each member introduces on an issue. Even in competitive congresses, members are rewarded for superior speeches on the issue, not merely for attacking a colleague's argument.

Student congress permits full deliberation. In traditional academic team debate, the order, number, and length of speeches are fixed, thus restricting consideration of the issue. In legislative debate, on the other hand, members deliberate for as long as they think necessary; the body determines when to end the debate. And although the assembly does put limits on speaking time, it can waive the limits. All of these features contribute to create an environment that seeks the best, not the quickest, outcomes.

Student congress encourages interaction among members. In formal academic team debate, personal interaction and exchange of ideas are limited: debaters address their opponents only in questions, and collaboration among team members is restricted by time constraints. Similarly, participants present their ideas only during designated speaking times. The legislative model, on the other hand, enables and encourages members to interact freely on two levels. First, during deliberation any member may seek clarification of statements, facts, or other issues that are pertinent to the motion at hand. In fact, some competitive assemblies reprimand and rank less favorably speakers who fail to recognize members seeking clarification. Second, members may informally discuss items with one another, lobby for support of their proposals, and work together to facilitate the overarching aims of the assembly. As noted above, even in competitive assemblies, there is no disincentive to cooperate.

Legislative rules of procedure allow for both structure and flexibility. All formal debate activities have rules governing their proceedings. Student Congress and other legislative debate formats often have extensive documents outlining procedures; one such document is *Robert's Rules of Order.*[10] In most debate settings, these rules cannot be changed during an event. However, legislative assemblies can modify their rules during sessions to ensure efficient conduct of business and respect for the basic principles of parliamentary procedure—the equal rights of all members and the right to courteous debate.

DISADVANTAGES OF THE LEGISLATIVE MODEL

The legislative format also presents some challenges for participants. Recognizing these common pitfalls helps you avoid them and is necessary for understanding the rules of procedure designed to address them.

One of the most common difficulties with this format is that participants may not come to the assembly with the knowledge they need to contribute fully. Because members introduce the issues, topics are wide ranging, and as a result, participants sometimes have difficulty preparing for the sessions. The best way to prepare is to research a variety of current issues of interest to your peers and your community so that you have the background to debate these topics and examine the merits of various solutions.

Maintaining quality debate can also be a problem. Even in competitive student congresses, participants may express views based on "feelings" rather than on critical thinking. In addition, when one position has overwhelming support, the issue may receive only minimal discussion, and voting may be based on unreasoned or "mob" support or rejection of a proposal. To avoid this problem, you should always find reasons for your positions that are beyond personal politics and feelings.

Size can also be a disadvantage. When a significant proportion of a large assembly wants to speak on an issue, proceedings slow down, and those indifferent to the topic lose interest. To compound the problem, the chair may not have the experience to ensure that everyone is included. Your hosts will try to avoid this problem by providing the chair with seating charts or some other mechanism that will enable easy monitoring of participation and recognition of all members in an equitable manner.

Finally, if you are new to student congress, you may find the rules of procedure intimidating. By familiarizing yourself with the principles underlying parliamentary procedure and learning how these are reflected in the rules, you can come to the assembly with a level of comfort that allows you to participate fully.

KEY CONCEPTS FROM CHAPTER 2

Characteristics of Legislative Assemblies

- Assemblies encourage full and free discussion to arrive at an opinion that the body as a whole will endorse.
- The entire assembly meets as a group with every member receiving an equal right to participation.
- Rules of legislative debate ensure that deliberations don't "stall" on a single issue.
- Members act on their own judgment, not predetermined positions.
- Each member's opinion is equal, as measured by a vote.
- Standing in disagreement does not affect rights to participate in the future.
- Even in the absence of some members, the assemblies' deliberations proceed as usual.

Advantages of the Legislative Model

- Participants make better decisions.
- Participants decide topics for discussion.
- Large numbers can participate.
- Members may argue for any position they choose on an issue.
- Assemblies promote collaborative decision making.
- Congresses encourage full deliberation of issues without regard to specific time limits.
- Congresses encourage informal interaction between members.
- Rules of procedure introduce a blend of structure and flexibility.

Disadvantages of the Legislative Model

- Preparation is sometimes difficult because of the format's spontaneity.
- Members often fail to critically examine issues, relying instead on reaction or emotion.
- Ensuring equal participation for everyone is often difficult.
- Rules may be unnecessarily intimidating.

NOTES

1. Henry M. Robert III, William J. Evans, Daniel H. Honemann, and Thomas J. Balch, eds., *Robert's Rules of Order*, Newly Revised, 10th ed. (Cambridge, Mass.: Perseus Publishing, 2000), pp. 1–2, l.8–17.

2. Ibid., p. 1, l.8–11.

3. Ibid., p. 1, l.12–14.

4. Ibid., p. 1, l.15–17.

5. Ibid., p. 2, l.1–3.

6. Ibid., p. 2, l.4–8.

7. Ibid., p. 2, l.9–10.

8. Ibid., p. 2, l.11–17.

9. The only time this is not so is when a large majority (traditionally two-thirds of the members present) determines that further discussion is either unnecessary or not germane to the goals of the parliament and those it represents.

10. Available online at http://www.constitution.org/rror/rror--00.htm. For the most up-to-date text and only *authorized* version of these rules, see Henry M. Robert III, William J. Evans, Daniel H. Honemann, and Thomas J. Balch, eds., *Robert's Rules of Order*, 10th ed. (Cambridge, Mass.: Perseus Publishing, 2000), pp. 1–2, l.8–17.

Section 2

Getting Started: The Basics of Student Congress

Chapter 3
Principles and Concepts of Parliamentary Procedure

This chapter offers background on some of the main principles of parliamentary procedure, introduces several key elements that are part of the vocabulary of parliamentary procedure, and describes some important parliamentary roles in student congresses. The principles this chapter outlines will help you understand the rules explained in later chapters. The discussion of elements and roles will help you understand how student congresses conduct business.

PRINCIPLES OF PROCEDURE

We can trace the parliamentary form far back into the history of representative government.[1] The characteristic fundamental to early assemblies was that participants met to discuss among themselves the values, principles, and courses of action they felt should be held in common. The importance of open deliberation to those affected by political decisions and the notion of such deliberations occurring in an ordered and representative fashion began to develop with the first political forums of Ancient Greece and Rome. Over the centuries it spread with varying degrees of success to emerging nation-states in Europe.

Gradually, the development of parliamentary procedure began to reflect the principles that form the basis of our contemporary parliaments and legislatures. These principles attempted to balance the rights and interests of all persons and coalitions in the assembly, including the following:[2]

+ the majority
+ the minority (especially a minority exceeding one-third of the total membership)

- individual members
- absentees

Balancing the rights and interests of all involved is still the foundational principle underlying the often complex rules governing all modern deliberative bodies. While the majority decides the will of the assembly, the procedures allow for a full discussion of any issue a member wishes to raise. Parliamentary procedure assumes the right of participation exists even when exercising that right may not be helpful to the body, for example, when a member expresses a viewpoint that other members find unreasonable or harmful. All individuals and coalitions have the equal opportunity to convince the majority of the virtue of their case. Discussing divergent viewpoints improves the critical evaluation of problems and ensures that the assembly is making the best decisions possible.

A second principle of parliamentary procedure is courtesy. Deliberations must be conducted in a civil manner. Members may become impassioned about an issue, but they must remember that they are debating issues, not people; motions, not motives. They should never impugn the integrity of a member or make other personal remarks.

A third principle requires that the assembly treat opposing viewpoints fairly. This not only means providing equal time for the opposition to speak but also acknowledging opposition voices. The principle of fair treatment allows assemblies to legitimately claim to express the will of the people through their representatives.

By adhering to these principles, legislative assemblies are able "to arrive at the general will on the maximum number of questions of varying complexity in a minimum amount of time and under all kinds of internal climate ranging from total harmony to hardened or impassioned division of opinion."[3]

Basic Concepts

Student congresses establish basic rules detailing who may participate, the form of their participation, and how business will progress. Many of the rules have vocabulary unique to their use, and therefore, we must define a few important concepts so that you can understand the rules you will learn about later.

Member

A member is a person who has the right to participate in all aspects of an assembly's proceedings, including the ability to make motions (i.e., bring matters before the assembly for discussion); to engage in debate about those motions; and to cast votes approving or rejecting them. Some assemblies include individuals who do not participate as members, for example, a professional parliamentarian, community observers, or others the assembly has invited to offer information or because they have an interest in the proceedings.

Rules of Order

Rules of order, or rules of procedure, are the formal written rules an assembly adopts as the guidelines for conducting business.[5] These rules maintain orderly deliberation and describe the responsibilities and privileges of the members and officers. The rules ensure smoothly running deliberations with definite procedures for dealing with disagreements. Most often an assembly's rules of order will include a basic text such as *Robert's Rules of Order*, on which the principles outlined in this chapter are based. But because parliamentary procedure is designed to help, not hinder, decision making, your assembly can modify the rules to fit its requirements or add rules it thinks important. These special rules of order supersede those in the basic text if the two are in conflict.

Rules of procedure are often written in extremely formal language. They can be challenging when you first read them, but their formality should not discourage you from using them. The language serves a purpose: the rules are meant to be dispassionate. They function as an objective reference when debates become heated. The following chapters present the essential rules and motions used in most student congresses in easily understandable language.

Decision Rules

Decision rules are procedures by which an assembly chooses to affirm or reject an issue or action that comes before it. Student congresses generally decide a question by majority vote of those members present and participating, but they can sometimes require a two-thirds vote to resolve an important issue. The distinction between those present and those participating in a vote is an important one, because it determines what constitutes a majority. For example, if 100 members are present, 90 vote and 10 abstain, only 60 votes would be required for a two-thirds majority vote. Choosing not to vote—abstaining—permits a member to not express consent or dissent and, in effect, to remain neutral.

Motion

A motion is the instrument used to bring business before the assembly. It is a proposal a member formally offers in a meeting that asks the assembly to take a specific action or express a particular opinion.[6] Motions may be simple oral statements or very formal written propositions. There are two major types of motions: main motions, which bring discussion before the congress; and secondary motions, which manipulate the main motion.

KEY ROLES

In addition, the members engaged in deliberation, the chair, the parliamentarian, and the judge are essential for a student congress. The following discussion provides an overview of their responsibilities.

The Chair

The chair plays an extremely important role in an assembly. This individual ensures that the body follows proper procedure, that everyone receives equal treatment, and that the assembly maintains a minimal level of order. Many assemblies elect one of their members to be chair as their first order of business.[7] However, in a student congress the three or four individuals who receive the most votes serve in the position for an equal amount of time. For example, in a six-hour student congress that utilizes three different chairpersons, each would serve for two hours.[8] In non-competitive context, the chair is often appointed, and the congress may ask a community member to serve. This is an especially good way to create connections with other community organizations and familiarize them with the concerns of the congress's representatives.[9]

The chair has several responsibilities. Her most important task is to act impartially when managing the assembly's deliberations. Motions, requests for recognition, and other items go through the chair, and the chair must ensure that everyone has the opportunity to speak for as long as the rules allow. Conversely, the chair must make certain that no member monopolizes speaking time on a motion or over the course of a meeting.

The chair also regulates the voting processes—calling for, counting, and announcing the vote—decides questions of order, and responds to parliamentary inquiries or points of information. If the chair is a member of the assembly elected to the position, the chair is entitled to vote. However, when the chair's vote would not affect the outcome, she commonly does not participate in the process. A non-member serving as chair has no vote.

Parliamentarian

The parliamentarian advises the chair on matters of parliamentary procedure. He offers his council, but the chair makes the formal rulings. The parliamentarian must be impartial and is a non-voting member. As a result, in most competitive student congresses the parliamentarian is drawn from outside the assembly, e.g., a co-host, coach, older student, unassigned judge, or other adult. This has the added benefit of developing outside relationships that can help the assembly in the long run. When the parliamentarian is unable to resolve an issue, the host becomes the final adjudicator of parliamentary conflicts.

Judge

In competitive student congresses, the judge evaluates the performance of each assembly member. She is responsible for assigning points for each speech a member gives based on the quality of arguments, the manner of presentation, and the overall contribution made to the assembly's deliberations. The judge also evaluates the performance of the chair, assigning points based on how well the chair attends to *all* the members needs, maintains a steady flow of debate, and settles disputes among participants. On some occasions, congresses may choose to use multiple judges.[10]

KEY CONCEPTS FROM CHAPTER 3

Principles of Procedure

- Assemblies attempt to balance the rights of all members and coalitions.
- Deliberations must be conducted in a courteous manner.
- Assemblies must treat viewpoints fairly.

Basic Concepts

- A member is a person with the right to participate in all aspects of the assembly's proceedings.
- Rules of order (rules of procedure) are the formal written rules for conducting the assembly's business in an orderly manner.
- Decision rules are the necessary action, e.g., majority vote, for arriving at a decision in the assembly.
- A motion is a formal proposal by a member asking the assembly to take a specific action or express a particular opinion.

Key Roles

- The chair moderates and ensures order in the assembly session.
- The parliamentarian advises the chair on parliamentary procedure.
- The judge evaluates the performance of members and the chair

NOTES

1. Henry M. Robert III, William J. Evans, Daniel H. Honemann, and Thomas J. Balch, eds., *Robert's Rules of Order*, Newly Revised, 10th ed. (Cambridge, Mass.: Perseus Publishing, 2000), p. xxvi.

2. Ibid., p. xlvii.

3. Ibid., p. xxvi.

4. Ibid, p. xxix.

5. Ibid., p. 15.

6. Ibid., p. 26, l.19–20.

7. The election of officers is discussed in depth in Chapter 5.

8. One way this rotation can be accomplished receives treatment in Chapter 5.

9. If a congress chooses to use a non-member as a chair, he or she would not be entitled to the voting privileges discussed for the chair.

10. See Chapter 11 for a detailed discussion of the judge's responsibilities.

Chapter 4
Motions

This chapter discusses motions, the tools used to introduce business in a student congress. It first examines main motions, which bring discussion before the congress. It then examines secondary motions, those motions that manipulate the main motion. These include subsidiary, privileged, and incidental motions. You will learn the specific characteristics that define each of these major categories. Finally, the chapter discusses motions that bring a question again before the assembly, commonly referred to as unclassified motions. These allow the assembly to change its previously adopted position on an issue.[1]

Main Motions

DEFINITION AND CHARACTERISTICS

A main motion introduces a topic for debate.[2] It proposes that the assembly take a certain action or express an opinion. Main motions are how the body conducts its work. Once a member has seconded a main motion, it becomes the focus of the assembly's discussion. Members may make motions to change it, but they may not offer other main motions until the body has voted on it.

Main motions have five major characteristics:[3]

1. A main motion requires a second. A member will offer a motion and another will "second the motion," indicating her support for discussing it.

2. Because main motions introduce an issue a member wishes discussed, they are always debatable.

3. To help the house build consensus on an issue, a main motion is always amendable.

4. A main motion always requires a vote. The assembly usually adopts a main motion by a simple majority vote, with only two exceptions: a main motion modifying a procedural rule requires a two-thirds majority, as does one to reverse previous action of the assembly.

5. The house may reconsider a main motion.

Five Characteristics of a Main Motion

- Requires a second
- Is always debatable
- Is always amendable
- Requires a vote
- May be reconsidered

Handling a Main Motion

When drafting a main motion, pay particular attention to the wording, because once the congress adopts it, the language becomes the official position of the assembly on an issue. A motion should be concise, unambiguous, and complete for the purposes it addresses. Motions may be short statements, for example, "I move that the assembly express its support for the War in Iraq." Alternately, they may be detailed and in the form of a written resolution or bill, in which case they often have titles (see Chapter 6). For example, "I move for consideration of the Prevention of Hate Crimes Bill."

As it works its way through the assembly, a main motion goes through a six-step process: three steps introduce it, bringing a topic before the house for deliberation; three dispose of it, leading the body to a vote on the issue.[4]

Introducing a Main Motion

The three steps introducing a motion are the following:

1. *A member makes the motion.* Any member can initiate this process. If no other business is being conducted, you may rise and, following the

chair's recognition, state your motion, for example, "I move that we consider adopting Prevention of Hate Crimes Bill." After stating the motion, you return to your seat.

2. *Another member seconds the motion.* The assembly cannot begin debating the motion until it is seconded. To second a motion, you simply say, "I second," or "Seconded." You do not have to obtain the floor. A second does not always imply that two members support the motion. Often individuals who oppose a motion will second it so that the house can debate it and ultimately go on record as rejecting it. A motion from a committee does not need a second. In this case a second is assumed because more than one member of the assembly is proposing it to the body. The assembly does not consider motions that do not receive a second. This rule keeps the deliberations running smoothly, because it ensures that the house will not have to devote time to an issue of interest to only one member.

3. *The chair states the motion.* Once a motion has been made and seconded, the chair states the motion. She may restate what the initiating member has said, read the motion if it is in writing and of manageable length, or, in the case of long motions, refer to it by title. The chair states, "It is moved and seconded that. . . ." After a motion has been moved and seconded, the individual making the motion may modify it and other members may ask for minor rewording. Members may also offer facts that prompt the motion's originator to withdraw it. However, once the chair has stated the question, members cannot modify the motion except by amendment.

Dispensing with a Motion

Once a member introduces a motion, the assembly goes through three steps in dispensing with it. These are as follows:[5]

1. *The assembly debates the motion.* Once the chair has stated the motion, she first offers the floor to the member who made it. Unless there is unanimous consent for the motion, debate then continues until every member has had the opportunity to speak. Typically, members may speak twice on a single motion, although the assembly may modify this rule. Any member seeking to speak more than once must wait until all members wishing to speak have had an opportunity to do so.

In most cases, congresses impose time limits on individual speeches, but the body may waive this rule under special circumstances.

The debate must focus only on the merits of the motion. Members should maintain a courteous tone and avoid personal attacks on other individuals and/or their motivations for taking a particular stand on the issue.

The chair has important responsibilities during the debate. Because she must maintain impartiality, she should not enter into the debate while presiding. Similarly, she should never interrupt the member speaking except when a breach of parliamentary procedure has occurred. The chair should facilitate the debate by alternately recognizing speakers in favor and opposed to the resolution

2. *The chair puts the question to a vote.* When the debate appears to have come to a close, the chair may ask, "Are you ready for the question?" or "Seeing no further debate, is the assembly ready for the question?" If no one seeks recognition at this time, the chair "puts the question before the assembly" after restating the original motion. The chair's wording becomes definitive; so if she has misread the motion, you may call a point of order to correct it. The wording is then entered in the minutes of the assembly.

3. *The chair announces the result of the voting.* Once she has read the motion, the chair calls for the vote. Assemblies normally vote by stating, "Yea" or "Nay," with the chair first calling for those in favor and then for those opposed. The vote is then recorded. If you feel that a vote has been improperly counted, you may call for a division of the assembly (see below). As a final recourse, but only in the case of highly contentious debates, you may request a roll call vote, in which the chair calls each member alphabetically and asks for a vote—"Yea," "Nay," or "Abstain." In the event of a tie, the chair may vote. When determining the outcome of the vote, only votes for and against, not abstentions, are considered. After the count is completed, the chair announces the result by stating the number of votes in favor and the number of votes opposed, and then announces whether the motion passes or fails.

Motions that have unanimous support do not have to come to a vote. In such cases, after a motion has been moved and seconded and the chair puts it to the floor, or after the debate, the chair may say, "If there is no objection to the motion, it may be considered approved by the assembly." At this point any member may object. If no one objects, the chair announces that the motion is approved by unanimous consent; if a member objects, the motion goes to a vote. A common example of approval by unanimous consent is the extension of speaking time. If the chair notices that a speaker is running short on time and that the house seems content to allow the member to continue, the chair may, at the end of the speaking time, say: "Time has expired. If there is no objection, the member's time will be extended by two minutes [pause]. Since there is no objection, the member's time is extended by two minutes." Unanimous consent does not mean that everyone supports the motion. Often, members opposed to a motion may consent to it because opposition would be futile and waste the assembly's valuable time.

Secondary Motions

DEFINITION AND CHARACTERISTICS

Secondary motions are those that members can make while a main motion is under consideration.[6] These motions affect the way the assembly will handle the main motion or address changes the house wishes to make to it.

All secondary motions share two characteristics:[7]

1. They can be made and debated while the assembly debates a main motion without violating the principle of considering only one question at a time.

2. When the chair has admitted a secondary motion as in order, the assembly must dispose of it before direct consideration of the main question can continue.

There are three classes of secondary motions: subsidiary, incidental, and privileged. (For a table of secondary motions, see Appendix 2.) These classes relate to their use in parliamentary procedure.

Introducing Secondary Motions

The steps for introducing secondary motions are similar to those for introducing a main motion. Secondary motions are usually made, seconded, and stated by the chair. However, unlike main motions, some may be made while another member has the floor on a pending main motion. The secondary motion then becomes the immediate pending question because, if adopted, it will affect the main motion. Once the assembly disposes of secondary motions, it may return to the main motion.

Under the rules of order, there are occasions when several secondary motions can be pending at the same time. In such cases, there is an order of precedence for dealing with them. The motions below are listed in reverse order of precedence. We present them this way so that you can see the order easily. Each type of motion takes precedence over the one before it: subsidiary motions yield to incidental, which yield to privileged.

Subsidiary Motions

Rather than simply adopt or reject a main motion, the assembly can use subsidiary motions to modify it.[8] The most common type of secondary motion, subsidiary motions have four characteristics:[9]

1. They are always applied to another motion and aid in dispensing with that motion.
2. They can be applied to any motion.
3. As a subclass of secondary motions, they fit into an order of precedence.
4. They can be made from the time debate begins until voting commences.

The use of subsidiary motions is limited by only two requirements: subsidiary motions must follow an order of precedence, and the motions must not be counter-productive or redundant. Subsidiary motions have rank, indicating the order in which the assembly must consider them. You can make a motion of higher rank when a motion of lower rank is pending. The higher ranked motion then takes precedence. We will discuss the specific subsidiary motions in reverse order of precedence; the last one discussed (motion to lay on the table) is highest in precedence.

Rank of Subsidiary Motions

Each motion in the table must yield to any motion below it.

Motion to Postpone Indefinitely

Motion to Amend

Motion to Commit or Refer

Motion to Postpone Definitely

Motion to Limit or Extend Limits of Debate

Motion to Previous Question

Motion to Lay on the Table

Motion to Postpone Indefinitely

This motion ends debate on a main motion and avoids a direct vote on it. The assembly uses it to dispense with a motion on which it does not want to take a position. The motion yields to all other secondary motions, and because it may only apply to a main motion, one must be pending when it is made. This type of motion may not be postponed or referred to committee; the assembly must vote on it immediately.

You can make this motion only if no member is speaking. It needs a second and is debatable. Debate may include the merits of the main motion because the motion to postpone indefinitely affects the final disposition of the main motion. You cannot amend this motion, since it calls for a very specific action: ending consideration of a main motion. This motion passes by a simple majority vote.

Motion to Amend

The most widely used subsidiary motion, the motion to amend allows the assembly to remove, add, or substitute items in the main motion.[10] Approval of this motion does not mean adoption of the main motion. Rather, once the amendment is accepted, the assembly considers the main motion in its modified form. If the house rejects the amendment, it continues considering the main motion in its original form. Members voting

Subsidiary Motions

Motion	Purpose	Second Required
Postpone Indefinitely	avoid a motion	yes
Amend	make changes	yes
Commit/Refer	create a committee	yes
Postpone Definitely	set debate for later time	yes
Limit/Extend Debate	limit consideration	yes
Previous Question	close debate; force vote	yes
Lay on the Table	postpone and consider other business	yes

for or against an amendment do not have to vote a particular way on the main motion.

Keep the following guidelines in mind when using the motion to amend:

1. All amendments must relate to the main motion. You cannot use a motion to amend to introduce a new subject. For example, if the assembly is considering a bill to combat multiple types of pollution, you could amend it to limit or expand the number of types, but you could not offer an amendment that addressed youth substance abuse.

2. You can apply a motion to amend to any main motion before the assembly. As you will see, you can also amend some secondary motions, such as the motion to limit or extend debate.

3. You can amend a motion to amend.

4. The assembly cannot refer to committee, postpone, or lay a motion to amend on the table. Once made, members must vote on it.

Debatable	Amendable	Required Vote	May Interrupt a Speaker
yes	no	majority	no
yes	no	majority	no
yes	yes	majority	no
yes	yes	majority	no
no	yes	majority	no
no	no	two-thirds	no
no	no	two-thirds	no

5. If the assembly postpones the main motion to which the motion to amend is applied, the assembly must first consider the amendment when it takes up the main motion again, unless another secondary motion of higher precedence was also postponed with it.

A motion to amend requires a second and is debatable. Approval requires a simple majority vote. Like the motion to postpone indefinitely, this motion is out of order when another member has the floor.

Motion to Commit or Refer
The motion to commit or refer can assign work to an existing committee or create a new committee to address an issue. This motion refers a main or secondary motion to a smaller group so that it can give the motion more intensive attention than it would receive in the full assembly. When made, this type of motion becomes the immediately pending question.

This motion is out of order when another member has the floor; it must have a second and is debatable. Because a motion to commit requires specific information, such as what the committee will be doing, the chair should not let deliberation on the motion proceed until the member offering the motion has supplied the information. During the debate, members may modify the motion in terms of who or how many members should be on the committee, what their responsibilities should be, and what the assembly expects the committee to produce. The motion requires a simple majority vote for adoption.

If the assembly is not satisfied with the committee's work, it can refer the issue back to the committee by following the same process and offering modified instructions.

Assemblies should use this motion cautiously. Because committee members will not be available for debate in the full chamber, the appointment of too many committees can limit the effectiveness of the main body and prevent members from speaking on motions of interest to them.

Motion to Postpone Definitely

This motion postpones debate on a main motion until a specific time (for example, 3:00 pm on September 30, or after all other business on the calendar for the session is complete). It is used when the assembly awaits information on a main motion; when the house wants to move more quickly through other items; or for some other reason the body determines appropriate, such as when a member interested in the issue under consideration is occupied with a committee assignment.

You can apply this motion to a main motion even if other subsidiary motions are pending. For example, a member may move to postpone definitely when the assembly is discussing a motion to amend. Once the congress approves the motion to postpone definitely, debate on the amendment and the main motion stop until the designated time. Once the designated time has been reached, the assembly then considers the motion to amend before returning to the main motion. You cannot make a motion to postpone definitely when another member has the floor, and it requires a second. It is debatable, but debate is limited to the merits of postponement, not the merits of the motion being postponed (as may occur when considering a motion to postpone indefinitely). You can amend a motion to postpone definitely to adjust the time when deliberation will resume. This motion requires a simple majority vote for adoption and may be reconsidered if it fails. However, if you want the assembly to reconsider the motion, you must present new justifications for a postponement. For example, if new amendments to a main motion make it more complicated and warrant a delay before deliberation continues, then a motion to postpone definitely may be reintroduced.

Motion to Limit or Extend Limits of Debate

This motion keeps debate moving efficiently. Typically, it reduces the number or length of speeches permitted under the congress's normal rules of procedure but does not immediately close debate. For example, it may limit each member to one speech on a motion and/or limit the time for each speech to five minutes. Alternatively, the motion may specify a later time, for example, 3:00 pm, after which debate will be closed and the question put to a vote. This motion can also permit longer speeches or give members more opportunities to speak. You can make it a main motion to become a general rule for an assembly or as a motion that applies to a specific subsidiary or main motion under consideration.

Because it keeps debate moving, this motion takes precedence over all debatable motions. You can apply it to any immediately pending motion or a series of motions. For example, you may apply it only to a pending motion to amend or you may apply it to the motion to amend and the main motion. You must specify what you want it applied to. Unless you do so, it applies only to the immediately pending motion. You can amend this type of subsidiary motion to adjust the limits it places on debate, for example, more or fewer speeches. If the assembly tables a main motion, it must take up the motion to limit or extend when debate on the main motion resumes. A motion to limit or extend requires a second and is not debatable. You cannot amend it except to change the original limits placed on the debate, for example, three instead of two more speeches. Because it limits the members' right to speak, it requires a two-thirds majority for adoption. This motion may be reconsidered only to include more speeches.

Motion to Previous Question

This motion closes debate and forces a vote on a question or series of questions. In most circumstances, you can apply it to more than one pending motion, i.e., a main motion and its related subsidiary motions. In these cases, once the assembly approves the previous question, it votes on each subsidiary motion in order of precedence and then votes on the main motion as affected by the subsidiary motions. This process can become unwieldy. You can make it clearer by applying this type of motion to the immediately pending question. Then, if desired, you can make it again for the next immediately pending motion. This allows the voting process to be broken up so that members are better able to keep track of which motion they are voting on. The motion to previous question is not a vote on a motion. Rather, it asks members to agree to stop debating and to vote on the motion. If accepted, the chair then states the question (or motion for which debate has been halted) and puts it to a vote, which determines its fate. You cannot make other motions until the assembly has dispensed with both the motion to previous question and the question (or main motion under consideration).

A motion to previous question takes precedence over all motions except the motion to lay on the table and incidental and privileged motions (see below). You can use it for any debatable or amendable motion. You may not make it while someone has the floor. The motion requires a second, but because it ends debate, it is not debatable or amendable. To ensure that a small majority is not denying a large minority the chance to speak, the motion requires a two-thirds vote for adoption. If it fails, debate continues. A member may reintroduce it later if that member thinks it will get the necessary two-thirds support. Voting one way on the motion to previous question does not dictate your vote on the question. Because this motion kills debate, you should make sure that everyone has had that opportunity to speak before introducing it. Remember, these and other motions exist to keep debate moving, not to deny others a chance to be heard.

Motion to Lay on the Table

This motion enables the assembly to put the pending question aside and temporarily address another issue. The chamber can leave a motion on the table as long as it chooses. It can also take up the motion for further consideration at any time, and when it does so, the motion takes precedence over any other questions. You should use this motion only if you want to revisit a question. If you do not want to consider a question, you can move to postpone indefinitely. The chair should call a member out of order if that member is obviously abusing this motion.

The assembly considers this motion before any other pending motion. When applied to a main motion, it includes all motions attached to the main motion, for example, a motion to amend. You cannot make a motion to lay on the table while another member has the floor. The motion requires a second and is not debatable or amendable. It needs a majority vote for adoption.

PRIVILEGED MOTIONS

Privileged motions deal with matters of immediate and overriding importance to the congress.[11] In many cases, they ensure equal participation. Because of their importance, they take precedence over other motions before the assembly: they may interrupt pending business and must be decided immediately, and they are not subject to debate.

Like subsidiary motions, these have an order of precedence that determines the sequence in which the assembly considers them. The discussion below examines them in reverse order of precedence: the first motion in this class yields to the next and so on.[12]

Rank of Privileged Motions

Each motion in the table must yield to any motion below it.

Motion to Call for the Orders of the Day

Motion to Raise a Question of Privilege

Motion to Recess

Motion to Adjourn

Motion to Fix the Time to Which to Adjourn

Motion to Call for the Orders of the Day

This motion requires the congress to adhere to the agenda established at the beginning of the session. It ensures that the assembly respects the priorities it has set. This motion is normally not needed unless the chair is inattentive to the original agenda or members are dissatisfied with adjustments to the schedule.

A motion to call for the orders of the day takes precedence over all subsidiary and main motions. However, it yields to other privileged motions

Privileged Motions

Motion	Purpose	Second Required
Call for the Orders of the Day	enforce agenda	no
Raise a Question of Privilege	attend to special needs	no
Recess	short break	yes
Adjourn	close and end debate	yes
Fix Time to Which to Adjourn	end assembly; set next meeting	yes

and the motion to suspend the rules (see below). You cannot apply it to any other motion, nor can you apply a subsidiary motion to it. This motion does not require a second because, like other privileged motions, it is designed to ensure that the body adheres to the principles of fair participation. You cannot debate or amend it.

This motion does not always require a vote. Once the motion is made, the chair renders a decision and implements the agenda. However, if a member objects, the chair must call a vote. Because this motion affects members' ability to participate, the assembly needs a two-thirds majority to reject the call. Once the house votes, it may not reconsider the motion unless there is a new infraction of the schedule. If the assembly accepts the call, all debate must end, and the congress returns to the original agenda. At this point, you can make any motion that is in order.

Motion to Raise a Question of Privilege
The motion for a question of privilege is used when members need to request a change not specifically related to the issue being deliberated. This type of motion is often used to make requests, find information,

Debatable	Amendable	Required Vote	May interrupt a speaker
no	no	chair's decision	yes, if necessary
no	no	chair's decision	yes, rarely
no	yes; time	majority	no
no	no	majority	no
no	no	majority	no

and inquire about other problems that may arise from time to time. If a member believes some minor change is in order, such as rearranging the seating to allow for better view of the chair, that member would move to raise a question of privilege. You may interrupt the speaker to make this motion, but do so only if the request is extremely urgent. This motion requires no second, is not debatable or amendable, and is decided by the chair. The assembly can reconsider it only if a member makes a motion to appeal. Motions to raise a question of privilege are rare.

Motion to Recess
The motion to recess calls for a short break in the assembly's proceedings and immediately interrupts the business at hand. It allows members to leave the chamber without missing business; the break generally lasts only a few minutes. Upon returning, the house immediately resumes its deliberations at the point it called the recess. Normally, the congress recesses to count ballots, find information necessary to continue deliberations, or allow for informal discussions. You can also offer a motion to recess as a main motion if no other motion is pending. Requests for a future recess

should be introduced as main motions so they do not interrupt the business at hand. Only motions demanding an immediate break are in order when another motion of any class is pending.

This motion takes precedence over all subsidiary and incidental motions as well as all privileged motions except those involving adjournment. You cannot apply it to any other motion and cannot move it when a member is speaking. Avoid motions for recess in the middle of debate; use them during slow periods, when they will be less disruptive. This motion needs a second. You cannot debate it, but you can amend it to change the amount of time granted for the recess. This motion requires a majority vote and may not be reconsidered.

Motion to Adjourn

This motion calls for the immediate close of business. You would use it, for example, if the congress had not scheduled a time for adjournment or if you wish to end the session before the scheduled time, even if business is pending. For example, if the orders of the day set adjournment at 4:00 pm and at 2:00 pm and you see that debate is going nowhere, you might want to move to adjourn. Often, the assembly adopts this motion unanimously. The motion need not prescribe a time to reconvene.

The motion to adjourn takes precedence over all subsidiary and main motions as well as all privileged motions except the motion to fix the time to which to adjourn (discussed below). However, it is out of order if the assembly is voting or if a member is speaking. You cannot apply this motion to any other motion nor does any motion apply to it. The motion must have a second and is neither debatable nor amendable. It requires a simple majority vote for adoption. The house cannot reconsider it, because no business may occur after adjournment. This motion is not necessary if the assembly's schedule indicates a time for the day to end. The chair can simply announce the adjournment at that time. To end the session after the scheduled time for adjournment has passed, you would call the orders of the day. Members may also request that the meeting continue by suspending the rules or moving to set aside the orders of the day (see below).

Motion to Fix the Time to Which to Adjourn

This motion is similar to the motion to adjourn but stipulates when the adjournment will end. It takes precedence over all motions except certain incidental ones, such as a point of order. Members may amend this element. The body may continue its business after approving this motion or, if it is at the end of the scheduled day, follow this motion with a motion to adjourn. Keep in mind that this motion does not end business; it merely stipulates when the assembly will meet again.

INCIDENTAL MOTIONS

Incidental motions relate to procedure and not directly to the question the assembly is deliberating.[13] Unlike subsidiary motions, which apply to any main motion while it is pending, these motions are only applicable under special circumstances. Some assemblies have numerous motions in this class, but student congresses commonly use the following five.[14]

These motions have no order of precedence. Typically, the assembly must decide them immediately before it can return to deliberations. Most of these motions are not debatable. The discussion below outlines the purposes and circumstances of their use.

Point of Order

If you think that the house is not following the assembly's rules of order properly, you may call a point of order. This requires the chair to make a ruling on a violation and enforce the rules. When doing so, rise and say, "Point of Order [followed by a brief explanation of the breach of rules in question]."

You can apply this motion to any violation of the assembly's rules. If the breach is of genuine concern, you can make this motion even when another member is speaking. It requires no second. Normally, this motion is not debatable. The chair will issue a ruling, after which the assembly continues deliberations. If the chair chooses not to rule and instead puts the question to the house, normal rules for debate apply. If put to the assembly, a two-thirds majority decides the question. A point of order is not amendable and cannot be reconsidered.

You should refrain from using this motion solely for technical accuracy. Use points of order only when a breach of the rules will fundamentally undermine the fairness of deliberations. When a breach occurs, you must raise a point promptly or the chair will consider the point too late for consideration because her ruling will have only a limited effect on the debate.

Incidental Motions

Motion	Purpose	Second Required
Point of Order	call for proper procedure	no
Appeal	dispute chair's ruling	yes
Suspend the Rules	relax procedure	yes
Division of Assembly	standing vote	no
Request and Inquiries		
1. Parliamentary inquiry	solicit chair's advice on rules	no
2. Point of information	question a speaker	no
3. Requests to withdraw a motion	remove a motion from debate	yes
4. Request for any other privilege	special uses	yes

The chair should either rule the point "well taken" or "not well taken." If well taken, the chair enforces the rule; if not, deliberation proceeds from the point at which it was interrupted. The chair should confer with the parliamentarian when making this decision. Members do not have the right to offer advice unless called on. If a breach is related to the debate over a motion and the congress has begun voting on it, you should avoid offering points of order, except in the most serious cases of abuse.

Motion to Appeal

The motion to appeal allows members to dispute a ruling of the chair on a matter of procedure. The assembly grants the chair the ability to rule on

Debatable	Amendable	Required Vote	May Interrupt a Speaker
no	no	chair's decision	yes
yes	no	majority	yes
no	no	two-thirds	no
no	no	automatic	no
no	no	no	yes
no	no	no	yes
no	no	majority	yes
no	no	majority, request based	yes

questions of procedure, vote verification, etc. However, any two members, by one moving and the other seconding, can require the chair to submit a ruling to the vote of the assembly. This is the only way you can dispute a decision of the chair.

This motion takes precedence over any question pending after the chair makes a ruling. You should make it before the assembly moves on to a new motion or other business. You can attach a privileged motion, for example, a motion limiting debate, to the motion to appeal. The privileged motion then takes precedence and must be resolved before determining the outcome of the appeal. You can appeal any chair ruling except points of order related to the debate on the appeal or when there is no reasonable alternative to the chair's decision. Remember that the chair's explanation of a ruling is not subject to the motion to appeal. You are not voting on the chair's rationale but on the ruling. You can make an appeal when another member is speaking; however, you must make it immediately following the ruling in question. This motion requires a second and is debatable but not amendable. Even if debate seems unwarranted, the chair has the right to explain a ruling before the house votes on the appeal.

Once debate has concluded, a simple majority vote overturns a chair's decision. A tie sustains the chair, and the chair may vote to create a tie. The vote is the final determination on the contested ruling. The house cannot reconsider the issue.

Motion to Suspend the Rules
The motion to suspend the rules is used to facilitate debate and further the goals of the congress. If the assembly wishes to do something that violates one of its regular rules, it can move to suspend the rules as long as such a suspension does not violate the basic rights of the members, such as their right to speak on the items of their choice. For example, an assembly commonly suspends the rules so that it can consider items in an order other than that on the agenda or to allow a member to speak longer without issuing a motion to extend limits of debate.

You can move to suspend the rules any time no other motion is pending. The motion to suspend also takes precedence over motions under consideration if it relates to them. It yields to privileged motions, except the call for orders of the day. You can apply this motion to any rule the congress observes, but you cannot apply subsidiary motions to it. Unlike other privileged motions, you cannot introduce it when a member has the floor. The motion requires a second but is not amendable or debatable. It requires a two-thirds vote for adoption and may not be reconsidered. If you wish to reinstate the rules, you must make a motion to that effect, essentially reversing the motion to suspend. Because of the confusion these changes may create, this motion should be specific and only make discrete changes, when possible. For example, a motion should include and explain the rule to be suspended, as in, "I move to suspend the rules so that the last item on the agenda may be considered immediately."

Motion for a Division of the Assembly

This motion is a very simple one that most assemblies use sparingly. It calls for a vote by show of hands so that the assembly can avoid a roll-call vote. You may call for a division after a vote, but you must make the motion before the congress moves on to the next question. This motion requires no second, allows no debate, and is not amendable. After the house adopts the motion, the chair immediately repeats the voting, but with the members raising their hands as the yeas and nays are called. The chair may also estimate the result. However, if the affirmative vote appears close, the chair should count it. Members have the right to appeal an estimation, and the chair must count any vote that requires two-thirds approval.

Request and Inquiries

You use this type of motion to request information or when you desire some other action that requires the assembly's consent. There are four common inquiries or requests, all of which take precedence over the motion with which they are connected. You can also make these without a motion pending or you can apply them to any other motion. However, you cannot apply a subsidiary motion to them. You can make these motions when a speaker has the floor only if they are immediately important. Two of the four, parliamentary inquiry and point of information, require no second; requests for permission to withdraw a motion and requests for any other privilege do. All four are not debatable or amendable. No vote is taken for parliamentary inquiry or point of information. The other two require a simple majority, although the votes are usually unanimous.

The following are the four common forms:

1. *Parliamentary inquiry*—This is a question directed to the chair about the congress's rules. Such questions help a member make an appropriate motion, understand the situation at hand or the effect of a motion, or raise a point of order. The inquiries must be germane to the business at hand and not hypothetical. When making this request, you rise and say, "I rise to a parliamentary inquiry." The chair then recognizes the inquiry by declaring, "The member will state the inquiry." You then state your question, for example, "Is it in order to call for the previous question at this time?" The chair's answer is an opinion, not a ruling, and is not subject to appeal. You may or may not act in accordance with the opinion, and may use points of order and the appeal process

to take any further action you think appropriate. Members should avoid using this motion while a member is speaking unless absolutely necessary. If you do so, the chair may defer addressing the point until the member has yielded the floor.

2. *Point of information*—These questions are related to substantive issues rather than procedure and are directed through the chair, even if the point of order is addressed to another member, for example, seeking clarification of the specifics in a speech. When requesting a point of information, you rise and state, "I rise to a point of information." If you are addressing it to the chair, the chair then says, "State the point," after which you state your question and the chair responds. If you are directing a question to another member, you say, "Will the member yield for a question?" If the member accepts the question, you ask it and retake your seat. The member then answers it, and the time it takes to answer is deducted from the member's allotted speaking time. A member does not have to accept a question, in which case he continues speaking. You can also use points of information to remind the speaker of an argument he should make or to rebut (make a point against) his argument. You must always state a point of information in the form of a question.

3. *Request for permission to withdraw a motion*—This request permits the member who introduced a main motion to withdraw it at any time after the chair has stated it but before the assembly votes on it. If you want to withdraw your motion, rise and state, "I ask permission to withdraw the motion." The chair can then ask for unanimous consent by saying, "Is there any objection to withdrawing the motion?" If the members have no objection, the motion is withdrawn. If a member objects, the chair can put the question to a vote or a member can second the request to withdraw, after which it is put to a simple majority vote. The question to withdraw overrides any subsidiary or incidental motions pending on the main motion. Once the assembly adopts the request, the question is dropped and the house may engage in new business.

4. *Request for any other privilege*—You use this motion when you wish to make a statement not immediately germane to the pending motion, for example, if you wish to make personal comments after a motion has

passed. You may make these requests when a member has the floor, but you should interrupt a speaker only if absolutely necessary. These requests are normally settled by unanimous consent. However, if a member objects, the assembly votes on the request using the normal procedure for a main motion.

Unclassified Motions

DEFINITION AND CHARACTERISTICS

The final class of motions reverses the actions of many of the motions discussed above. These motions are sometimes referred to as unclassified since they don't fit into the logic of many of the other motions.[15] They fulfill the parliamentary dictates that the assembly cannot address the same question twice without special procedure and that it cannot take action that prevents it from taking up business it postponed. They are important because they allow an assembly to remain flexible and attentive to the changes that occur as the body deliberates. There are three of these motions.

Motion to Take from the Table

This motion brings back before the congress a motion it has laid on the table. The motion takes precedence over no other motion, and therefore you cannot make it while another motion is pending. You can apply it to any motion laid on the table as long as the assembly has considered at least one other motion since the earlier one was tabled. If the motion to take from the table fails, you must wait until the house has considered another motion before attempting your motion again. You may not introduce it when a member is speaking, but you may signal the chair by rising and moving to the area of the room from which individuals deliver speeches or by passing the chair a note that you intend to make this motion. You must make this motion before the assembly considers another motion. A motion to take from the table requires a second but is not debatable or amendable. It passes by a simple majority vote and can only be reconsidered as described above. You make this motion by rising and saying, "I rise for the purpose of moving to take the question from the table." The chair then puts your request to a vote.

Unclassified Motions		
Motion	Purpose	Second Required
Take from the Table	bring back before assembly a motion laid on table	yes
Rescind or Amend Something Previously Adopted	adjust text of an adopted motion	yes
Discharge a Committee	remove question from further committee consideration and bring it to full assembly	yes

Motion to Rescind and Motion to Amend Something Previously Adopted

A motion to rescind strikes out a paragraph, several paragraphs, or an entire motion that the assembly has adopted. A motion to amend something previously adopted does precisely that. Both are handled in the same way. You must introduce them when no business is pending, because they take precedence over no motions. You can apply them to anything the congress has adopted, i.e., motions, bills, resolutions, etc. Similarly, you may apply all the secondary motions to them.

You cannot make these motions when another speaker has the floor, and they require a second. Debate over it may consider the merits of the motion it will affect. You can make amendments consistent with the rules for the motion to amend. Because these motions change a previous decision of the body, a two-thirds vote is required for adoption. And it may be reconsidered if it fails.

You can call for reconsideration of these motions at any time, and you do not have to vote as you did during their original consideration. You make the motion by rising and saying, "I move to rescind the resolution

Debatable	Amendable	Required Vote	May Interrupt a Speaker
no	no	majority	no
yes	yes	two-thirds	no
yes	yes	majority	no

related to, or titled, [state the adopted motion that the motion to rescind will affect]." To amend, you say, "I rise to amend the motion related to, or titled, [insert information to identify motion in question] by inserting and/or removing [information to be changed]."

Motion to Discharge a Committee
This motion removes a question from further committee consideration and brings it to the full congress. It is useful because as long as the question remains with the committee the assembly cannot take up an issue that involves the same subject matter or goals. Thus, this motion allows the congress to address questions in committee before a session ends.

You can make this motion only when no other motion is pending. It can apply to any committee and any item the committee is considering. All secondary motions, such as motions to amend or limit debate, may be applied to it. You cannot interrupt a speaker to make this motion, which requires a second. Debate over it may consider the merits of the question it wishes to call back before the assembly. The motion may request a committee report immediately or at a specific time, at which time the congress must consider the question even in absence of a report. You can amend the motion with regard to the time the congress will take back the question. Like all motions that change a previous decision, it requires a two-thirds vote for adoption. This motion, like the motion to take from the table, requires only a majority vote.

You make the motion by rising and saying, "I move that the committee established to investigate the subject of . . . (or the motion regarding . . .) be discharged." If you wish, you may include a time for the committee to report its findings. The motion referred to the committee then becomes the assembly's immediate business.

- The motion is the basis of deliberation in the legislative setting.
- Main motions introduce business.
- Secondary motions make modifications and control the form of the deliberation.
- There are three classes of secondary motions:
  - Subsidiary—help dispose of a main motion
  - Privileged—deal with matters of immediate and overriding importance to the assembly
  - Incidental—relate to procedure and not directly to the question the assembly is deliberating
- Unclassified motions allow the assembly to reconsider its previous decisions.
- Each type of motion relates to the others according to an order of precedence (rank): subsidiary motions yield to incidental, which yield to privileged.
- Subsidiary and privileged motions have a rank in which they must be considered. You can make motions with a higher rank while a motion of a lower rank is pending.
- Incidental motions have no order of precedence.
- Each motion relies on specific rules for its use, and its effect is governed by similar rules.

NOTES

1. While this chapter offers a brief overview of the motions, you may also wish to consult *Robert's Rules of Order*. The work is available in print or on line at http://www.constitution.org/rror/rror-05.htm#33.

2. Henry M. Robert III, William J. Evans, Daniel H. Honemann, and Thomas J. Balch, eds., *Robert's Rules of Order*, Newly Revised, 10th ed. (Cambridge, Mass.: Perseus Publishing, 2000), pp. 95, l.1–99, l. 20; pp. 108, l.1–116, l.3.

3. *RONR* (10th ed.), p. 59, l. 23–35.

4. Ibid., p. 31, l.4–7.

5. Ibid., p. 40, l.28–31.

6. Ibid., pp. 56, l.12–59, l.15.

7. Ibid., pp. 56, l.30–57, l.10.

8. Ibid., pp. 121, l.1–210, l.20.

9. Ibid., p. 62, l.1–23.

10. See Chapter 8 for a detailed discussion of amendments.

11. *RONR* (10th ed.), pp. 211, l.1–239, l.6.

12. These privileged motions, sometimes referred to as privileged questions, should not be confused with questions of privilege, which we will be discussed shortly.

13. *RONR* (10th ed.), pp. 240, l.1–288, l.6.

14. Readers wishing to learn more about these concepts can refer to *Robert's Rules*.

15. *RONR* (10th ed.), pp. 289, l.1–324, l.36.

Chapter 5
Meeting in Session: Procedures in Practice

This chapter gives you an overview of how a basic student congress session functions.[1] In previous chapters you learned about the principles and concepts that underlie parliamentary procedure and how assemblies conduct business using motions. Now you will see how many of the principles and concepts are put into practice. The chapter first discusses what happens during the meeting of a competitive student congress—establishing a roll and electing officers. Then, it describes how an average meeting day might unfold, and presents the rules covering major aspects of the proceedings—obtaining the floor, debating, voting, and adjourning.

OPENING THE ASSEMBLY

This section reviews the actions taken at the beginning of most student congresses. It centers on the administrative steps that any assembly, large or small, formal or informal, takes to ensure that the rules are implemented easily and efficiently.

Registration and Establishing a Roll of Members in Attendance

While in most competitive student congresses entries are solicited prior to the day of the tournament, you or your coach may need to enter your name on a roster or sign a position on a seating chart. Registering is important because it allows for the efficient conduct of subsequent business. The seating chart or roster facilitates roll-call votes and enables the chair to keep track of speakers.

Convening and Host Remarks

Once the registration period has ended, the congress is convened. Usually, this occurs when all members have arrived and found their seats. If required by the rules of the congress, participants are then sworn in. The host notes any changes to the agenda, special rules, or other considerations important to the day's deliberations and usually makes a few introductory remarks. She also may introduce the parliamentarian, announce whether there will be one or multiple chairs, and explain the judging process. In a non-competitive congress the host may play less of a role in the beginning of the assembly: welcoming members; reminding them of any pertinent themes of the assembly and rules for deliberation; and introducing non-members the host has helped recruit from community organizations to participate in the congress.

Nominating and Electing the Chair and Other Necessary Members

The congress's first order of business is electing the chair. Until this happens, no other business can take place. The host or some other person the organizers have chosen presides over the election. Members of the congress nominate candidates. The acting chair or host records these nominations, offers each nominee a chance to explain why he or she seeks the position, and oversees the balloting. After the voting is completed, the acting chair counts the ballots and announces the winner. The nominee with the majority of votes assumes the chair. The person conducting the election also records the names of the two nominees with the next highest number of votes. One of these individuals acts as chair if the winner steps down for any reason, including joining the debate. If the congress uses multiple chairs over the course of the session, the runners-up will act as the chair after the tenure of the first candidate expires. In the case of multiple chairpersons, each should serve for an equal number of hours. For example, in a six-hour session with three chairpersons, each would serve for two hours. Many student congresses have found rotating the chair extremely useful because it gives participants the opportunity to experience the legislative model from a different perspective. Since the position calls for impartiality, an individual never acts as chair while engaging in debate.

The Session

After the officers are in place, the chair calls the congress to order and asks for motions. Early in the proceedings, the assembly should adopt a motion for a schedule, unless organizers have provided one. The schedule should outline the topics the body will address at what time and indicate when breaks will occur. You may also want to offer other motions to set time limits for speeches or to limit the number of speeches on a motion. As you learned in Chapter 4, you can always extend or reduce the number, if necessary. After this process is complete, the chair begins recognizing members who wish to obtain the floor.

Sample Session Schedule	

9:00 am	Registration (9–9:30)
	    Establish Seating Chart or Roll of
	    Participants in Attendance
	    Take Nominations for Chair
	    Elect Chair
	    Call to Order
	    Adopt Agenda

10:00 am–1:00 pm	Regular Business Begins
	    Floor is open to motions*
	    Members may introduce bills,
	    resolutions, etc., as motions during this
	    time

1–2:00 pm	Midday Recess
2–5:00 pm	Regular Business Continues
4–5:00 pm	*If necessary, this time in the regular schedule can be set aside to take up postponed or committee-referred motions*
5:00 pm	Adjournment of the Assembly

*Whether motions come from an agenda or from the members on the floor depends on the nature of the agenda adopted. The agenda is only the initially prescribed order.

Obtaining the Floor

The chair must recognize a member before he or she can speak. This recognition "gives the member the floor"—the exclusive right to speak at the time he is recognized. To claim the floor, rise when no one has it, and say, "Madam (or Mr.) Chair." If you are entitled to the floor, the chair will recognize you by name, if possible, or she will clearly indicate that you have the floor by pointing to you or calling you to come to a certain area of the assembly's room. (If the chair does not recognize you by name, give your name to her so that she can acknowledge you explicitly.) You then remain standing and speak for as long as the rules permit. When you are finished, you yield the floor by retaking your seat.

If two members rise at the same time, the member who gains the chair's attention first has the floor. While another member has the floor, you may not rise in an attempt to gain future recognition. Similarly, you may not interrupt a speaker while that person has the floor, except under circumstances outlined in the rules of procedure. However, the chair can interrupt a speaker if that person has breached the rules or is not addressing the motion at hand.

Assigning the Floor

The chair uses the following rules to assign the floor during debate:

1. The member who makes a motion has the right to speak first.

2. A member may not have the floor twice on the same question until all those wishing to be recognized have spoken once.

3. If rules 1 and 2 do not apply, the chair assigns the floor so that debate alternates between support and dissent. (If the assembly is not divided on the motion, the chair may continue recognizing speakers until interest expires or a member moves the previous question.)

The chair should keep track of who has been speaking on any given motion so that each individual speaks once before a member speaks again. The chair should also note who has spoken a great deal that day and give preference to members who have not.

If you think that the chair has recognized someone out of order, you may call a point of order to object, but you should not abuse this rule. The decision of the chair on issues of recognition is final.

Courteous Debate

One of the key principles of legislative debate is courtesy. Members must be able to debate even the most contentious issues in an atmosphere in which members respect each other. The principle of courtesy enables the body to focus on issues rather than on personalities and motives. There are several steps you as a member can take to ensure courteous deliberation.

1. *Address all remarks through the chair.* This is a basic rule of parliamentary procedure. Even if you have a question for another member, you must address it to him through the chair. For example, "Madame Chairman, how does the member suggest we raise funds for the new youth center he is proposing?"

2. *Address members by title rather than by name.* For example, "Madame Chairman," rather than "Jean"; "the member who offered the amendment," rather than "Joe." This formality keeps the focus on the issue rather than on the individual.

3. *Focus on issues rather than personalities and motives.* Never make an *ad hominem* attack against a member who disagrees with your position. You may question the efficacy of someone's proposal, but you may never question a member's motives.

4. *Do nothing that intentionally impedes the business of the assembly.* Avoid offering dilatory and improper motions. You must not use parliamentary procedure to obstruct business just because you don't like the way things are going.

Expediting Business

Because the goal of student congress is to discuss a wide variety of issues, the chair should do everything possible to expedite business. The chair can do this in several ways.

1. *Know the assembly's rules.* Although the chair can consult the parliamentarian, business will move more efficiently if the chair has a clear understanding of the assembly's rules of procedure.

2. *Use general consent whenever possible.* Voting takes time. If the chair believes that the assembly is in agreement on an issue, or if the house is conducting routine business, the chair may ask if the members have no objection to adopting the motion. If no one objects, the motion

is adopted, but if even one member objects, the chair must put the motion to a vote. The chair can also develop a consent agenda to consolidate routine business and dispose of it at one time, rather than having the congress vote on each element separately.

3. *Keep the focus on motions.* Occasionally, members who have the floor may attempt to deliver a speech rather than offer a motion. If this happens, the chair should politely phrase the speaker's theme as a motion and ask if that is what the speaker intends by his speech.

4. *Restate the motion if the debate wanders.* If a member begins discussing a tangential or different subject, the chair should remind the member of the motion on the floor.

5. *Deal quickly with dilatory motions.* Dilatory motions are those used to hinder rather than facilitate business. The chair should rule them out of order or refuse to recognize members who use these tactics.

Voting

Voting can often be one of the most time-consuming parts of a legislative assembly. It can cause problems in student congresses that meet only once or on an irregular basis, because time spent on voting takes valuable time away from the main goal: debating issues. Most competitive congresses have no way to hold over issues from one session to another, since the members may only meet once or their composition may fluctuate based on competitor interest in a given tournament. Thus, issues they do not have time to consider will be dropped. On the other hand, some non-competitive assemblies meet on a semi-regular basis, which allows some continuity in topics or the holding over of topics of interest until the next meeting. In either case, the assembly should move through the voting process quickly so that time can be focused on deliberation.

Voting follows a standard procedure. The chair calls for a vote any time debate expires, for example, when individuals are not interested in continuing debate on a motion, or when the assembly has adopted the motion to move the previous question. At that point the chair states the motion, for example, "The vote is on the motion to amend." The chair may also wish to clarify what a vote in the affirmative (yea) and negative (nay) means, for example, "Voting for the motion to amend will strike the following wording: '. . .'; and add as follows: '. . . .'" The chair then calls for a voice vote: "All

those in favor, please say yea (pause); all those opposed, say nay (pause)."
The chair then announces her judgment of the vote and records it in the
minutes.

If a member thinks that the count may not be accurate, that member
may move for a division of the house. In this case, the chair asks members
to signify their vote by a show of hands. Again, the chair counts and records
the vote. The chair will sometimes ask members to stand while voting even
if there has been no request for a division of the house. Members may have
been distracted when the vote was called, and asking them to rise for the
vote not only allows the chair to count the members more easily but also
helps ensure that everyone knows that a vote is occurring.

When an issue is heated or extremely important, you may want to move
for a roll-call vote. You must do this immediately after a vote by vocal acclamation or division of the house and before the congress has moved on to
other business. The motion is not debatable or amendable and requires a
majority vote for acceptance. If the motion fails, the assembly considers
the vote by show of hands or division final; if it carries, the chair reads the
roll in alphabetical order and asks each member to state his or her support (yea) or dissent (nay) for a motion. This procedure ensures that each
individual's vote is accurately counted. In most instances, a roll call is not
necessary.

Adjournment

Adjournment marks the end of the meeting. The time is usually set in the
schedule, but as you learned in Chapter 4, a member can move to adjourn
before that time, even if business is pending.

You might want to move to adjourn if you feel that debate is getting
you nowhere, or if you need more time to review important information.
Alternately, members may request that the meeting continue by suspending the rules or moving to set aside the orders of the day if the assembly is
involved in vigorous debate.

Adjournment can take place without a motion. If the chair announces
that the time for adjournment has arrived and no one moves to set aside
the orders of the day, the meeting may be adjourned by declaration. The
assembly can also adjourn before the scheduled time if it has finished the
schedule. In this case the chair will ask if there is any more business, and
if there isn't, the chair will declare the meeting adjourned. However, most

competitive student congresses sessions fill the scheduled time. This is particularly important in National Forensic League congresses in which the rules require that sessions meet for a minimum number of hours.

As you recall from Chapter 4, you can use several motions to adjourn. You can move to adjourn, which closes the meeting without setting a time for reconvening; you can move to fix the time to which to adjourn, which prescribes the conditions for the congress to reconvene; or you can move the orders of the day, which forces the congress to abide by the scheduled time for adjournment. Remember, the meeting is not adjourned until the chair declares it adjourned.

KEY CONCEPTS FROM CHAPTER 5

The Opening Meeting

- Establishing a roster is important for conducting business.
- The congress's first order of business is electing the chair.

The Session

- Deliberations begin after officers are in place.
- The congress should adopt a schedule early in the session.
- The chair must recognize a member before he can speak.
- Steps to maintain courteous deliberation include the following:
  - Address all remarks through the chair
  - Address members by title rather than by name
  - Focus on issues rather than personalities and motives
  - Do nothing that intentionally impedes the business of the assembly
- The chair can expedite business by:
  - Knowing the assembly's rules
  - Using general consent whenever possible
  - Keeping the focus on motions
  - Restating the motion if the debate wanders
  - Dealing quickly with dilatory motions
- Move through the voting process quickly.
- Voting may be by vocal acclamation, show of hands, rising, or roll call.
- Adjournment can take place without a motion, or members can use several different motions to call for adjournment.

NOTE

1. This chapter outlines general procedures for how most student congress sessions are conducted. However, congresses may vary. You should contact the host or review the rules of the specific assembly to determine the procedures the congress you participate in will follow.

Section 3

Participating in Legislative Debate: Introduction to Key Activities

Chapter 6
Calling for Change: Writing Your Resolution or Bill

This chapter introduces two common types of main motions: resolutions and bills. It begins by defining these motions and discusses the questions you must consider in preparing them. It then explains how to use your preparation to create these motions and put them in the proper format.

DEFINITIONS
Resolutions and bills are main motions in written form. Resolutions indicate a position a member wants the congress to take on an issue. A resolution is a simple statement of support for, or disagreement with, a policy, event, or other issue. A bill sets policy and identifies specific actions needed to implement it as well as penalties involved in noncompliance.

CONSIDERATIONS FOR RESOLUTIONS AND BILLS
Resolutions and bills isolate a specific problem and state a specific response based on observation of the problem. For example, a resolution may recognize the lack of after-school programs for young people and suggest that the congress express its support for more programs. A bill, on the other hand, may go one step further and establish a specific type of program.

Before you write your resolution or bill, you must have a clear understanding of the problem you face and the action you want to take. To do this, you must take four steps.

1. *Clearly articulate the problem and research its causes and effects.* For example, if you want to address the problem of substance abuse among young people, you would explore what experts say are its causes— parental influence, poverty, peer pressure, etc. Not all experts agree,

so you would have to research a wide range of literature from various fields. You must also investigate the effects of substance abuse, again casting your research net broadly.

2. *Determine the scope of the problem's impact.* How many people are affected? Do they have common characteristics? Is there an environmental or situational scope to the problem? In the case of substance abuse, you would want to discover how many young people are substance abusers, what substance abusers have in common, and whether substance abuse has led to increased crime and physical deterioration of neighborhoods. This research will determine how you shape your resolution. For example, if you find that substance abuse affects only a small group in one neighborhood, you might call for a more highly targeted response than if you discover the problem involves a significant proportion of young people throughout a city, state, or country. Your research and critical thinking will help you make this decision.

3. *Think critically about why the congress should act on the problem.* You may find this difficult to answer because the need to act can seem obvious. However, you will have to persuade your fellow participants that the issue is worth their time and effort. To do so, you must convince them not only that the problem you address is serious, but also that your resolution will solve it. Sometimes benefits are as simple as a reversal of the problem and its effects. For example, if your solution decreases substance abuse, it will probably contribute to reducing vandalism and neighborhood deterioration.

4. *Develop a clear vision of how you want to solve the problem.* You must explore what experts and members of your community think, and examine actions that have succeeded in other areas. You also need to determine how a congress can best implement such actions. For example, are substance abuse abatement programs most effective when administered by a local or state government or more directly in schools or at community centers? Your vision must also include the specific ways such a policy can be enforced. For example, you may call for the establishment of a new government office to develop an after-school program. By creating resolutions and bills that identify specific policies or problems, you help ensure that your thinking about social issues parallels the concerns faced by government legislators. This is

beneficial for both your own critical thinking and your understanding of public problems.

With the background you need and a clear vision of what you want to accomplish, you are now ready to draft your own bill or resolution.

What to Include in Resolutions and Bills

As you have learned, resolutions are short documents that declare a position you want the assembly to adopt while bills describe a policy you want the body to enact. You should frame your resolution or bill around the items discussed in the previous section so that it is responsive to the problem you believe the assembly should address.

Purpose and Form of Resolutions

As you now know, resolutions ask the congress to take a position on an event, problem, policy, or other issue of importance. In order to convince the assembly to adopt your position, you present your rationale in a series of "whereas" statements that describe the problem, give a sense of the scope of its impact, and present the reasons why the assembly should adopt your position. In some cases, you may also want to discuss the benefits of the assembly taking a position on the issue.

Keep the reasons for adopting your position brief. Each statement should be no more than one or two sentences. Brevity is important for two reasons. First, you will be elaborating on your premises in the speech you deliver when offering the resolution and in the debate that follows. Second, because members frequently amend resolutions, keeping the key points concise makes the resolution easy to understand and facilitates the amendment process. Focus your resolution on the position or action you want the assembly to take. You can use more and longer clauses to describe what you wish the assembly to do because this is the key portion of your motion.

A resolution has a simple format that contains only three elements:

1. A title that describes the subject you are addressing, e.g., "A Resolution of Support for Pollution Programs in Our Community."

2. A list of the reasons underlying it. These are offered in a series of "whereas" statements that present the premises that support the conclusion your resolution draws or action it suggests.

3. The position or action you wish the assembly to adopt.

Basic Form of a Resolution (without benefits)

(TITLE)

Whereas (*insert observations about the causes and effects of the problem your resolution addresses*);

And, Whereas (*if more premises are necessary to describe the problem, continue to add them; if not, the next set of clauses should explain the scope of the problem*);

And, Whereas (*after completing the clauses describing the problem and its scope, the next set of clauses should be those outlining reasons the resolution should be acted on*);

Therefore, Be It Resolved, by the Student Congress here assembled, that [position or action the assembly should take].

Alternatively, a list of benefits is optional. If you think your resolution needs more extensive justification, you can add a benefits portion after your statement of position or action. Remember, the quality of a resolution is based on content, not style.

Basic Form of a Resolution (with benefits)

(TITLE)

Whereas (*insert observations about the causes and effects of the problem your resolution addresses*);

And, Whereas (*if more premises are necessary to describe the problem, continue to add them; if not, the next set of clauses should explain the scope of the problem*);

And, Whereas (*after completing the clauses describing the problem and its scope, the next set of clauses should be those outlining reasons the resolution should be acted on*);

Therefore, Be It Resolved, by the Student Congress here assembled, that [position or action the assembly should take].

Insomuch as we believe this action should be to the benefit of our community, the present resolution offers the following benefits:

First, (*insert an independent benefit of your position*).

Second, (*insert a second independent benefit of your position*).

Third, (*insert a third independent benefit of your position*).

The following is a simple resolution, with only a few premises and benefits. Yours may be longer or shorter. The complexity of the issue you address will help you determine how to draft your resolution.

A Resolution Concerning the Environment of Our Communities

Submitted by: Thomas Seville

Date: June 27, 2007

Whereas pollution is having a significant impact on the quality of our community and the health of members of our community;

And, Whereas this pollution affects the quality of life and potentially the health of all of us along with the long-term welfare of our environment;

And, Whereas this problem deserves our action both for the immediate benefits it offers and the long-term commitment that we hold to protecting the environment that we share;

Therefore, Be It Resolved, by the Student Congress here assembled, that we initiate cooperation with local recycling programs in such a way as to increase the presence of waste disposal and recycling facilities throughout our communities and especially in the schools we attend.

Insomuch as we believe this action should be to the benefit of our community, the present resolution offers the following benefits:

First, this will lead to a direct improvement in the natural beauty of our community, which is currently tarnished by the unsightly waste in our streets and parks.

Second, this will improve the environment around the schools we each attend every day.

Third, this will ensure that the environment that is crucial to our community is sustainable in the long term by reducing excess waste through recycling efforts.

Purpose and Form of a Bill

As you have learned, the purpose of a bill is slightly different from a resolution. Because bills are motions that, if enacted, carry the force of law, they must be definite, include specific actions that can or cannot be taken, and include penalties for not complying so as to give the legislation force. While you will not be passing real laws, thinking about policy issues in similar ways is why student congress offers such useful insights into real political controversies.

Like resolutions, bills include a few basic elements that you should include regardless of the topic you address. The basic structure of a bill includes four elements:

+ A title that describes the subject matter you are addressing, e.g., "A Bill to Increase Pollution Control"

+ A section identifying the specific policy the bill will enact if passed

+ A section identifying what, if any, conditions limit the bill's enforcement

+ A section that explains the means of enforcement, i.e., what are the consequences of non-compliance

---

Basic Form of a Bill

(TITLE)

Be it enacted by Student Congress here assembled, that:

Section 1. (*Here you identify the specific policy your bill would enact if passed by the congress*).

Section 2. (*You next identify any exceptions to its enforcement or other nuances of its enactment*).

Section 3. (*Finally, you include the enforcement clause in which you articulate what the consequences of non-compliance will be*).

Sample Bill

A Bill to Increase Pollution Control

Submitted by: Thomas Smith

Date: June 4, 2007

Be it enacted by the Student Congress here assembled, that:

Section 1. All cities and any other local political units, e.g., townships, will establish a community-based recycling program that will provide environmentally friendly disposal of common waste products, including, but not limited to, paper, plastics, glass, and aluminum.

Section 2. Only when one or more of the following conditions are met, may any city be relieved of the obligations to promote the recycling efforts outlined in section 1 of this legislation:

A. The economic burden of such a program would interfere with other social programs deemed of overriding importance, e.g., health-care provisions, education, etc.

B. The economic burden of such a program would interfere with the provision of adequate public safety, e.g., police, fire, emergency management, etc.

C. The political unit in question has already established a similar program that is achieving measurable progress toward a reduction of pollution.

Section 3. Any locale found in violation of this legislation, either by failing to establish a program or misrepresenting the program, will face fines of up to $1,000,000 and/or possible audit by an external entity.

Introducing Your Resolution or Bill

Once you are ready to present your resolution or bill, you introduce it as a main motion (see Chapter 4). You do this by rising and, when recognized by the chair, saying, "I rise to move the adoption of the resolution [state the title of the resolution or bill]." After you motion is seconded and open for debate, you deliver your speech in support of your resolution. We will discuss how to do this in the next chapter.

KEY CONCEPTS FROM CHAPTER 6

Definitions

- Resolutions indicate a position a member wants the congress to take on an issue.

- Bills enact a policy to solve a problem the congress has identified.

Considerations for Resolutions and Bills

- Have a clear understanding of the problem you face and the action you want to take:

  - Articulate and research the problem

  - Determine the impact

  - Determine why the assembly should act on the problem

  - Develop a clear plan for solving the problem

What to Include in Resolutions and Bills

- Frame your resolutions and bills around the four elements of analysis presented above.

- When writing a resolution,

  - Keep the premises, the justifications for your resolution short

  - Focus on the position or action you want the assembly to take

(continues)

KEY CONCEPTS FROM CHAPTER 6 (*continued*)

- A resolution contains three elements:
  - A title describing the subject
  - A list of reasons underlining the resolution
  - The position you wish the assembly to adopt

    A list of benefits is optional
- When writing a bill,
  - Frame your policy in very specific language to limit confusion;
  - Consider the workability of its implementation and account for it in any exceptions you articulate;
  - Include an enforcement clause that considers how to most effectively enforce such a policy.
- Bills contain four major elements:
  - Title
  - Statement of Policy
  - Exceptions to the Policy
  - An Enforcement Clause
- You can modify the form of a resolution or bill to suit your needs.

Chapter 7

Moving Others to Act: Writing Your Speech of Advocacy*

Speeches often form the basis for decisions, as they are a means of persuading individuals to adopt one course of action over another. This holds true not only in student congresses but also in the daily opportunities you have to express your views to others. This chapter teaches you how to organize your thoughts, put them into words, and present them in a persuasive manner. With this background and with practice, you will have the tools necessary to be an active participant and a positive influence in a student congress.

PREPARING TO WRITE A SPEECH
Before writing a speech you need to consider the following questions:

+ What is its purpose?
+ Who is the audience?
+ What is the setting?
+ How can you best respond to the diverse viewpoints of your audience?

Purpose
You must define the purpose of your speech before composing it or you risk rambling from one unrelated topic to the next. Listing your goals helps

---

*Brian Danielson and Michael K. Middleton

you clarify your thesis and organize the arguments and proofs to support your position. The following questions will help you clarify your goals.

1. *What is the specific problem that you want to address?* Often, you need to narrow the scope of your speech when dealing with a broad or multifaceted problem. For example, while you could address pollution in general, you may be better off focusing on one type of pollution so that you can provide your audience with an in-depth analysis. Or you might want to talk about the impact of various types of pollution on a specific locality or species. Limiting your speech to the specific impacts allows you to better organize it into a coherent and persuasive text. Remember, the key is to keep your speech as focused as possible.

2. *Whom does it harm? How many are harmed?* Answering these questions will help you articulate the significance of your topic. If you can make the issue important to society in general and your audience in particular, you can keep your speech from becoming boring and ineffective.

3. *What should be done about it?* Answering this question is a vital component of any speech. Simply stating a problem without offering a solution is irresponsible. If you identify a problem, you are obligated to suggest what to do about it. Public speaking enables individuals not only to highlight a problem and its dimensions but also to propose solutions to it. When recommending a solution, you should make sure that your audience has the ability to implement it.

   For example, if the resolution or bill you are addressing focuses on the issue of water pollution, you would inform your audience about the sources of pollution, the amounts and types of pollutants entering the water, and the impacts of that pollution. At the same time, as a responsible citizen, you would also propose reasonable measures for reducing local water pollution. You might suggest that the congress vote in favor of stringent fines on polluters, ban toxic runoff, and increase the number of water treatment plants in the community. Ultimately, the solution you propose should be reasonable given the political situation.

Audience
Identifying your audience enables you to focus your speech on those aspects of the issue important to your listeners. In doing so, your speech becomes

more persuasive and motivates your audience to adopt your solution. When trying to define your audience, ask yourself the following questions:

+ What does your audience do for a living?
+ What is their socioeconomic position, i.e., are they rich and powerful, middle class, poor?
+ Where do they live?
+ What sort of group affiliations do they have?

These questions, along with many others, will enable you to determine what arguments will be most effective.

Let's continue with the water pollution example. The arguments that you would use in a speech to your local business association would be different from those you would present to a group of concerned parents. Addressing the business people, you would discuss how pollution hurts your community's economy. For example, tourists won't visit a polluted place. On the other hand, if you were addressing a group of concerned parents, you would talk about how water pollution is harmful to children's health.

Thinking about who your audience is also helps you develop potential solutions. You might suggest to businesspeople that they employ the latest technology to clean their wastewater before releasing it into local rivers. You might encourage parents to lobby local government to tighten regulations on dumping toxic substances or to join environmental organizations that lobby government on the issue.

Your peers in a student congress will be most likely to support your bill or resolution if you speak to their concerns. For example, your speech should stress the effects of pollution on their specific communities, or discuss the long-term effects of pollution on the world they will live in. The more relevant you can make your argument to their concerns, the more successful you will be.

Setting

Setting refers to the forum for your presentation, the time constraints placed on it, and the social context in which you give it. Answering the question of setting is relatively easy when addressing the forum and time constraints, but becomes more difficult when examining the social context. Let's deal with each of these issues separately.

The forum in which you will give your speech is one of the key elements you must address, because the tone of your presentation should change with the venue. For example, your speech should be more formal when addressing the entire assembly than when speaking to a small group in committee.

Time constraints are also important when preparing your speech. Often, you will have only a very limited time for your presentation. The old adage "So much to do and so little time" is just as applicable to speech making as it is to the rest of life. In student congresses you sometimes have only three minutes to speak; therefore, you must plan carefully so that you can present all your major points before your time expires.

You want to speak just long enough to "get the job done." In other words, you should take the time you need to persuade your audience, and speak not a moment longer. Think of when your teacher droned on about a concept that you, and everyone else in the class, fully understood. You probably became bored, stopped paying attention, and ceased to care about what he or she was saying. Your audience will react the same way to an excessively long speech.

Considering the social context of your speech is important as well. Often world events have a direct link to the issue on which you are speaking. Understanding how these events relate to your topic is important for several reasons. First, knowing the social context of the issue can help you research your speech. For example, if you know the details of the Kyoto Protocol on global warming, you could use that information as background for your speech on air pollution. Likewise, knowing the social context may impact your solution directly. For example, if you know that legislatures in your community will be debating pollution control in the near future you might find it useful to suggest the audience write their representatives to urge adoption of the protocol in an effort to help solve the problem.

Diversity

Your audience will often include people from a wide range of backgrounds with different worldviews. You must consider these differences when preparing your speech. More important, however, you should identify similarities between yourself and members of your audience. This enables you to tailor your speech so that your audience can identify with your argument and conclusions. Indeed, many of the world's famous speeches addressed values and principles that bridged differences in understanding and background.

WRITING YOUR SPEECH

Now that you have thought about the issues of purpose, audience, setting, and diversity, you are ready to write your speech. You might be a bit apprehensive about the process. Rest assured, if you have written a paper, you can write a speech. Writing the speech involves three steps: organizing it, researching the necessary information and incorporating your findings into your presentation, and addressing stylistic concerns.

Common Organizational Structures

First, a disclaimer. There is no such thing as the "correct" way to structure a speech. As long as the audience can follow your logic and the speech is persuasive, it is a good speech. However, there are two common organizational structures you can use to make your speech effective. If this is your first speech, use one of these as a template. Once you have a working outline, play with the structure until you feel it is right. Remember, no one writes speeches in stone; after you have outlined your speech, you must go back and edit the outline until you find what works for you.

The most common structures used for speeches of advocacy are known as Main Reasons and Problem–Solution. Both allow you to organize your arguments in a logical fashion. The basic components of both are similar; they are just arranged in a different order.

Main Reasons Structure

The basic format of the Main Reasons structure is as follows:

I. Introduction—This portion of the speech draws attention to the problem that you are addressing. Commonly, the introduction grabs the attention of the audience with statistics that clearly demonstrate the significance of the problem, the story of an individual who has been affected by the problem, or a parable. This section of your speech should be short; in a three-minute speech the introduction should last about 15 to 30 seconds. The point is to introduce the audience to the problem, make them want to hear more about it, and set the stage for the rest of your speech.

II. Thesis—Following the introduction, you should state your thesis—the course of action that you want the audience to adopt. Make this short: one or two sentences.

III. Preview/Transition—This section outlines the order of your speech. Commonly, the preview/transition section is worded as follows:

> In order to prove that we should adopt (*the course of action put forth in the thesis*), I will demonstrate in the following three areas why it would be beneficial to do so. First, (*first problem/benefit*). Second, (*second problem/benefit*). And third, (*third problem/benefit*).

Although the Preview/Transition section of your speech is short, it is vital, because it ensures that the audience can follow your arguments.

IV. Body—The body constitutes the largest portion of your speech. In a three-minute speech, you should allocate approximately two to two and a half minutes to it. Generally, you should organize the body around three reasons, or subpoints, for adopting the action in your thesis. Each of the subpoints should provide an independent justification for accepting your thesis. Don't worry if you don't have exactly three; there is no rule that says you must have that number. However, you should remember that your audience's attention span is limited; therefore, present no more than four or five of your strongest subpoints.

One of the common ways to support the thesis is to use each of the subpoints to identify one aspect of the problem that you are trying to solve and then explain how the course of action you propose would solve it. For example, if you were giving a speech that advocates reducing water pollution, you might present the following subpoints:

1. Water pollution kills large numbers of fish and other sea life that are an essential source of food. You would talk about how pollution affects fish, how increases in pollution correspond with decreases in fish stocks, and how many people rely on fish as a major source of food. Then you would explain how adopting your course of action would lead to decreases in species loss.

2. Water is essential to human life. You would describe how pollution affects drinking supplies and present statistics on the number of people who get sick or die from contaminated water. Then you would explain how adopting your proposed action would lead to better drinking water.

3. Pollution destroys the natural beauty of our environment. You would describe how pollution turns rivers and lakes into eyesores, how it creates more nuisances for community members in the form of pests, and how it drives away species by devastating their environment. Then you would describe how your plan remedies those problems.

V. Conclusion—This section wraps up your speech. In it you remind your audience of all the reasons they should accept your thesis. Keep in mind, this part of your speech should only summarize your key points and not introduce new ideas. Often speakers will undercut their speech's effectiveness through a rambling attempt to tie their ideas together in the conclusion.

Problem–Solution Structure

The Problem–Solution structure follows a slightly different format than the Main Reasons structure.

I. Introduction—The introduction in this model serves the same function as in the Main Reasons structure. It presents a problem and sets the stage for your presentation.

II. Preview/Transition—This section has same purpose as in the Main Reasons structure: to inform the audience of the order of your presentation. The wording would generally be as follows:

> Today, I would first like to inform you about the problems associated with (*policy X*); next, I will propose a solution to the problems; and finally, I will explain the benefits of making the change.

III. Body—The body of the Problem–Solution structure is composed of three separate sections: a problem, a solution to that problem, and the benefits of the solution. This structure is particularly useful in the legislative context because it implements a basic persuasive model. At the end of your speech, your audience should recognize the problem you have articulated, understand how your solution addresses it, and be able to identify benefits that ought to encourage their acceptance of your position.

    A. Problem—In this section, you outline the problem you want to solve, and provide multiple examples of ways that the problem affects individuals.

    B. Proposed Solution—This section serves the same function as the thesis portion of a Main Reasons structured speech. However, in this structure you can provide more detail about how the policy works, what sorts of resources it requires, and what other individuals support or have supported similar solutions.

    C. Benefits—This portion of the speech explains how the proposed solution will lead to a variety of benefits. Often this section links each benefit to a specific aspect of the problem you outlined earlier.

IV. Conclusion—This portion of the speech serves the same function as the conclusion of a Main Reasons structure.

These two structures can serve as guides to writing your speech. You may choose one or the other—or some combination of the two.

Research

You may be wondering why we are discussing research in a chapter on speech writing. That's simple: gathering evidence to support your arguments is essential to writing a good speech. But shouldn't you have finished your research before you start writing? To some extent this is true; you should have completed the vast majority of the research before outlining your speech to ensure that your ideas aren't based purely on bias. However, once you have decided on the goal for your speech, you must continue your research to strengthen your overall argument, fill in gaps in your logic, and refine the appeals you use.

Once you have outlined your speech, you will be able to direct your research in a more productive manner. Remember our water pollution example? Once you have determined the basic structure of your argument, separating the strong arguments from the weak, all you have to do is find additional evidence that supports the argument you are trying to make. For example, the second argument about why we should work to reduce water pollution is that it can lead to human suffering and death. In order to support this argument, you would need to find three main pieces of evidence. First, you would have to find information that explains the ways in which water pollution affects drinking water supplies. Second, you would need to find statistics that document the number of individuals who die or who become sick each year as a result of water pollution. Finally, you would need to find some evidence that supports your solution. Once you have found evidence to support that particular point, all you have to do is repeat the process for each of the remaining portions of the speech.

Your research might also go beyond your topic. You might want to find speeches that you think are particularly well written or compelling to glean ideas about how to stylistically "jazz up" your presentation. Look at how others have used repetition, metaphors, alliteration, and other elements of good public speaking to call their audiences to action. Many of the best speakers have learned their craft by modeling their speeches after those that have resonated through history.

Practicing and Editing

You are not finished with your speech once you have a draft. You must edit it and practice it again and again. These two processes are interconnected. As you practice, you will discover where you need to edit, and then you must practice—and perhaps edit—again. You cannot ignore these steps. And you must repeat them over and over if you are to give an effective speech. Practicing seven or eight times is usually a minimum for effectively delivering a short speech. During a legislative session, you may not have enough time to do this, but you should practice as many times as possible.

Remember to practice your speech as you will perform it. Do not rush through it. You should speak at the same rate as you would in normal conversation. If you have difficulty delivering certain phrases or if they sound awkward, change them. At this stage, don't worry about time limits. You will notice that as you become more comfortable, the time you take to deliver your speech will diminish. However, if you are still over time after several readings, you should shorten it.

After you have smoothed out the rough edges, present the speech to a friend, a parent, or a teacher. This will help you overcome any nervousness you might have about speaking in public and will serve as a great source of ideas during the editing process. Because you have been deeply involved in researching your arguments, you might think they are clear and compelling, while others might find them confusing. Having someone else listen to the speech can help you clarify your arguments before you are on center stage. You might also try switching the order of your arguments. Sometimes, when you hear the arguments in a different sequence, they will make more sense or improve the speech. Keep practicing until you feel comfortable. You'll know when you're ready.

GIVING YOUR SPEECH

When you give your speech, make sure that you have an outline with you. Occasionally, no matter how many times you have practiced, you might forget a phrase, a sentence, or even a whole argument. If you have a fairly detailed outline, you can easily get back on track and deliver your speech with confidence. Be careful that your notes or outline don't distract you or your audience. Keep them discretely hidden in your hand or on a lectern.

Finally, you may find yourself in a situation in which you will not be able to use a prepared speech. If so, you can use the outlines above to guide you as you sketch your spontaneous arguments. As long as you follow one of these structures, engage in rigorous review of your outline, and use it to guide your speech, you may find that with experience your off-the-cuff comments can be even more compelling than your prepared presentations.

KEY CONCEPTS FROM CHAPTER 7

Preparing to Write a Speech

Before writing a speech you need to consider:

- purpose
- audience
- setting
- diversity

Writing Your Speech

There are two common organizational structures:

- Main Reasons
- Problem–Solution

Research

- Research is important for developing sound ideas based on facts rather than bias.
- You must continue to research after outlining your speech to strengthen your overall argument and fill in gaps in your logic.

Practicing and Editing

- Your speech is a work in progress. You must repeatedly edit and practice.
- More practice is always better; your goal should be seven rehearsals, when possible.
- Presenting your speech to a friend or teacher will help you overcome your nervousness and refine your arguments.

Giving a Speech

- Make sure you are comfortable with your material.
- Speak at a normal, conversational speed.
- Use an outline to aid your memory.

Chapter 8
Creating Common Ground: Preparing Amendments

Next to offering main motions and giving speeches for and against them, offering amendments and speaking for and against them is the most common type of participation you will encounter in student congress. This chapter will familiarize you with the uses and implementation of the amendment process. It begins by describing the occasions when amendments are part of debate. Then it presents factors you should keep in mind when preparing an amendment, and explores how you construct it. Finally, the chapter gives you an overview of how to guide your amendment through an assembly.

Occasions for Amendment

Amendments attempt to improve an original motion. Most often they are a means of honing a resolution or bill, but they can be used to refine secondary motions as well. Amendments are most commonly used for six purposes.

1. *To refine or change the action or position proposed by a resolution or bill.* This type of amendment alters the action or position in an original motion. For example, if a resolution calls for increasing the number of landfills to deal with the problem of solid waste, you might introduce an amendment calling for stringent recycling procedures rather than more landfills.

2. *To expand or limit the scope of a resolution.* This use makes actions the assembly is considering more reasonable by adjusting their scope. For example, if a member offers a motion calling for expanded security at the main entrance to the train station, you might offer an amendment

calling for more security at all entrances. Or if a member introduces a resolution aimed at combating pollution, you might offer an amendment limiting the proposed action to a single type of pollution. This type of amendment is useful in making sure assemblies undertake manageable projects and programs.

3. *To add items to a resolution.* This type of amendment supports a resolution but takes it one step further. For example, if a resolution is focused only on recycling efforts to combat environmental problems, you might offer an amendment to expand the efforts to include more responsible use of resources.

4. *To remove items from a resolution.* If you think that the resolution you are addressing includes an action that is redundant, unnecessary, or unmanageable, you can offer an amendment to remove it. For example, if the congress is debating a resolution to publicize water pollution control measures on radio, television, and the Internet and you think that using television might be too expensive, you could offer an amendment to strike television from the original motion.

5. *To substitute items.* These amendments accept the underlying purpose of a resolution or bill but argue that the effort should be directed elsewhere. For example, a resolution might call for the congress to develop a program of increased relations between the government and media organizations. You might agree with the premise but think that it is best to bypass the media and create direct relationships with schools, community organizations, and other groups. You would then offer an amendment substituting your position for the original.

6. *Facilitate the manner in which the assembly conducts itself.* Often motions, such as those to extend debate, are amendable in terms of the time. For example, you may feel that deliberation is going nowhere. In that case you might offer an amendment limiting debate to 30 more minutes.

Considerations in Preparing Amendments

You should consider two questions when preparing an amendment and the speech you will give presenting it: why is the amendment needed and what are the implications of the change?

To answer the first question, you must articulate the reasons for the change that the amendment will offer: why, for example, should the scope of a resolution be narrowed or broadened? Just as important, you must explain why the amended resolution or bill is superior to the original. To do this, you have to describe the advantages the amendment brings to the resolution or point out the disadvantages of the original bill that the amendment avoids.

To answer the second question, you must determine the precise effects of the change you want to make and how that change will affect the motion. For example, an amendment to a resolution imposing controls on landfills that calls for stringent recycling procedures might require the creation of more recycling facilities and development of an ad campaign so that citizens understand the new rules. Thus, such an amendment would change the intent of the original motion.

After you have answered these questions, you must identify the wording in the original motion that you want to change, and adjust the text. Do this step carefully: make sure that your wording clearly articulates your intent.

STYLE OF AMENDMENTS

Amendments are relatively short documents that contain only four elements:

1. A title that reflects the change the amendment seeks to make, for example, "An Amendment to Expand the Efforts to Combat Water Pollution."

2. The portion of the original resolution or bill the amendment will change. If your amendment substitutes a clause for one in the original resolution, for example, you would quote the affected clause. If you were adding or subtracting a clause, you would indicate where in the document the amendment will make the change.

3. The wording of the change the amendment makes. If the amendment is an addition or substitution or some other change, the new phrasing would be indicated in quotation marks. If it is a subtraction, this portion would be blank.

4. The type of change being made. To ensure clarity, you identify the type of change: addition, subtraction, or substitution.

Basic Form of an Amendment

(TITLE)

Submitted by: (Your name and, if applicable, your supporters' names)

Date: (date submitted)

Original text or identify where addition or subtraction is to be made:

New text:

Type of change:

Now let's apply the style to a specific amendment. First, we present a sample bill. Then, we show how it could be amended.

A Bill to Increase Pollution Control

Submitted by: Thomas Smith

Date: June 4, 2007

Be it enacted by the Student Congress here assembled, that:

Section 1. All cities and any other local political units, e.g., townships, will establish a community based recycling program that will provide environmentally friendly disposal of common waste products, including, but not limited to, paper, plastics, glass, and aluminum.

Section 2. Only when one or more of the following conditions are met, may any city be relieved of the obligations to promote recycling efforts outlined in section 1 of this legislation:

A. The economic burden of such a program would interfere with other social programs deemed of overriding importance, e.g., health-care provisions, education, etc.

B. The economic burden of such a program would interfere with the provision of adequate public safety, e.g., police, fire, emergency management, etc.

C. The political unit in question has already established a similar program that is achieving measurable progress toward a reduction of pollution.

Section 3. Any locale found in violation of this legislation, either by failing to establish a program or misrepresenting the program, will have to face fines of up to $1,000,000 and/or possible audit by an external entity.

Amendment That Has Won Assembly Approval   **(The new text is bolded for the sake of clarity.)**

Title: An Amendment to Limit the Bill to Increase Pollution Control

Submitted by: Joseph Johnson

Date: June 6, 2007

Original text or identify where addition or subtraction is to be made:

"Section 3. Any locale found in violation of this legislation, either by failing to establish a program or misrepresenting the program, will have to face fines of up to $1,000,000 and/or possible audit by an external entity."

New text:

Section 3. Any locale found in violation of this legislation, either by failing to establish a program or misrepresenting the program, will have to face fines of up to "**$500,000**" and/or possible audit by an external entity.

Type of change: Substitution

For Chair's use:

Accepted: (X)   Rejected: ( )   Vote (Y/N): 57/30

GUIDING AMENDMENTS THROUGH THE ASSEMBLY

If you wish to introduce an amendment to a motion, you should deliver it to the chair at a time when you will not disrupt deliberation—during a break or between speeches, for example. Then, when no member is speaking, rise and say, "I move to amend the main motion with the motion previously submitted to the chair entitled ('*Insert your title here*')."

Once your move to amend has been seconded, you as the author are entitled to give a speech supporting the amendment. Much of the argument you make will address the considerations suggested in this chapter. Remember to use the speech-making skills you learned in Chapter 7. At the end of that debate, the assembly will vote on the amendment, and the chair will record the outcome on the amendment form. If the assembly accepts your amendment, the debate will return to the main motion in its modified form; if it rejects the change, debate will resume on the original main motion or will be open to other secondary motions related to the main motion.

KEY CONCEPTS FROM CHAPTER 8

Occasions for Amendment

Amendments are generally used for six purposes:

1. To refine or change the action or position of a resolution or bill
2. To expand or limit the scope of a resolution
3. To add items to a resolution
4. To remove items from a resolution
5. To substitute items
6. To facilitate the manner in which the assembly conducts itself

Considerations in Preparing Amendments

You must consider two questions when preparing an amendment:

1. Why is the amendment needed?
2. What are the implications of the change?

Style of Amendments

Amendments contain four elements:

1. Title
2. Original text of the affected motion
3. New text of the affected motion
4. Type of change

Guiding Amendments through the Assembly

- Present you amendment to the chair at a time that does not disrupt debate.
- To make an amendment, rise when no one has the floor, and say, "I move to amend the main motion with the motion previously submitted to the chair entitled (*insert title*)."
- As the author of the amendment, you are entitled to speak first on its behalf.

Chapter 9
Resolving Difference/Taking Action: Participation in Committees

One common way student congresses refine ideas and come to an agreement on a position or action is to use committees. Committees can also help carry out the wishes of the larger assembly. This chapter first examines the benefits of using committees. Next it discusses how and why committees are formed. Finally, it describes how they deliberate and come to decisions.

BENEFITS OF COMMITTEES

Student congresses form committees for several reasons.

1. *To refine their position on a specific issue.* Frequently, congress members hold a wide range of viewpoints that cannot be easily reconciled in a large body. By moving the discussion to the more informal committee setting, members representing various viewpoints can more easily find a compromise. For example, you and your fellow members may be interested in taking a position on water pollution but disagree on what that position should be. Some want to stop industry from dumping hazardous chemicals into rivers, while others want to increase the number of water treatment plants. By moving the issue to a committee formed of representatives of all positions, the various sides might come to mutual agreement on the issue, in this case, perhaps using fines from companies that violate dumping regulations to construct water treatment plants.

2. *To gather information and opinions on an issue.* The assembly may form a committee to investigate an issue and report its findings. These reports may be purely informational or they may advise the congress on how to proceed on an issue. For example, a committee research-ing substance abuse among young people may write an informational report outlining the scope of the problem in the community. In this case the assembly determines how it wants to act on the committee's report. Alternately, if the committee is asked to come up with rec-ommendations, it may find that after-school programs are effective in dealing with the problem and recommend that the assembly fund such programs.

3. *To develop a resolution or bill expressing the will of the congress.* Often, the congress may be interested in a topic but does not have enough information to act on it. In this case, it might form a committee to investigate and develop a resolution on the issue. For example, mem-bers may decide that pollution is a problem on which the congress should act, but they do not know precisely how. The congress would then form a committee to investigate the issue and develop a motion on which it could act. The committee might investigate the most prev-alent types of pollution, what are the causes, what are the effects, what are possible solutions. Based on its findings, it might then develop a resolution calling for stringent recycling. The committee then returns that motion to the assembly for deliberation. This type of committee process greatly expands the ability of the congress to act on a variety of issues

Forming Committees

When forming committees, the congress must consider several questions. The first is, what is the committee's purpose? This may range from infor-mation gathering to reaching a compromise on behalf of the larger body. Next, the congress must define the results it expects. This might be an amendment to a motion, a report distilling information the committee has gathered, or a resolution or bill on which the assembly will act.

Questions to Consider When Forming Committees
• What is the committee's purpose?
• What results are expected?
• Who will serve on the committee?
• How big will the committee be?

The congress must then determine who will serve on the committee. A committee should provide a cross-section of the views in the assembly. This is particularly important when the congress is forming a committee to resolve an issue raised in debate. Ensuring that committees include all the major perspectives is the best way to guarantee that the compromise the committee develops is agreeable to the congress as a whole.

The next issue is the committee's size. Two factors are important in determining this. First, the committee needs enough members to handle its appointed task. Unless the committee has adequate personnel, it may not be able to fulfill its mandate, or the results it produces may be unsatisfactory. In determining numbers, the congress must also consider the impact that committee formation will have on the functioning of the main body. Remember, individuals on committees will not be in the larger assembly as deliberations continue. The congress must balance the benefits of having a large committee against the problems created by having a large portion of the members unavailable for debate.

DECISION MAKING IN COMMITTEES

Decision making in committee is far more casual than it is in the main assembly. Because committees are often small, as few as three people, they do not need to use the formal procedures that govern the larger congress unless the committee members think them useful.

Yet all committees must abide by two rules. First, they must appoint a chair so that one person serves as the committee's representative when reporting back to the assembly. Second, committees must vote on their final product—be it information, a resolution, or some other item—and report that vote to the congress. Other items, such as minutes, may prove useful but are undertaken at the discretion of the committee and the congress.

Strategies for Decision Making

Once the committee is formed, it must determine the strategy it will use to make its decisions. Two are presented here. Keep in mind that these are guides. Your committee should use the decision-making process that best helps it fulfill its mandate.

Standard Agenda Process

The standard agenda process is a six-step procedure for decision making designed to ensure that all the aspects surrounding a decision receive due attention.[1] The following steps comprise this process.[2]

1. *Identify the Problem.* The congress's directive to the committee will help determine this, but the committee will also have to decide the specific aspects of an issue that need to be investigated if it is to fulfill its goals. For example, if the committee is addressing the issue of pollution, it might determine that it should investigate only air pollution or various types of pollution in a specific location.

2. *Analyze the problem.* Once the committee has identified the problem, members need to gather specific information so they have a clear sense of the factors that affect the issue and the possible solutions. For example, if a committee is looking for ways to improve opportunities for disadvantaged young people, it must determine who is affected, what the effect is, what solutions have/haven't worked, and what are the other aspects of the issue.

3. *Determine the criteria against which solutions will be evaluated.* Members next establish what criteria they will use to evaluate suggested solutions. For example, the committee may decide that the resources available to implement a solution are a major consideration in developing a resolution or bill on helping disadvantaged youth. Does the congress have the time or the means to implement the solution? Another criterion may be whether the solution achieves a specific goal. The more criteria committee members can develop, the easier it will be for them to determine a solution agreeable to all.

4. *Generate possible solutions.* In this step, members present a wide range of solutions so that they can weigh each against the others. Depending on the committee's goals, each member might draft a few resolutions or amendments or write a report summarizing information the committee has gathered. Many of the solutions may have emerged in previous steps, but this step ensures that all possibilities are formally laid before the committee, so the members can evaluate each in a systematic manner.

5. *Evaluate the solutions and select the best.* This step is relatively easy if the committee has followed the other steps. Using the criteria developed in step 3, committee members discuss the advantages and disadvantages of each solution and select the two best options. The committee then votes on the most beneficial—the solution with the greatest potential advantages and minimal disadvantages based on the committee's criteria.

6. *Implement the solution.* Depending on its mandate, the committee may offer a new motion to the congress for debate, introduce an amendment, or present a report on an issue. If the congress has asked the committee to initiate contact with media or community outlets, implementation may include executing plans to gain public awareness of and support for the congress and its activities.

Nominal Group Technique

The nominal group technique is also a six-step decision-making process in which members engage in a series of deliberations that gradually narrow the possible solutions to the best available.[3] Unlike the standard agenda process, this approach encourages group refinement of ideas and endeavors to include as many solutions as possible. Consequently, voting replaces evaluation according to predetermined criteria. Here are the six steps:

1. *Generate ideas.* After the committee has defined and analyzed the problem, members individually develop possible solutions.

2. *Compile ideas.* Each idea is written on a chart so that members have a comprehensive list of all the possible solutions.

3. *Discuss ideas.* The committee discusses each idea so that members have a clear understanding of the proposal and its implications.

4. *Vote on ideas.* The committee votes to narrow the solutions. Each member gets to vote once for a limited number of solutions. For example, members might vote for no more than three-fifths of the total number of choices. If there are five motions, then each member may vote for three. Only those solutions that receive a vote from the majority of committee members are continued for discussion.

5. *Discuss narrowed list.* Members discuss the ideas that received majority votes.

6. *Continue narrowing options.* Members repeat steps 4 and 5 until one solution remains.

Neither of these two models is better than the other. You and your fellow committee members can combine any of the steps you find useful, or use another model with which you feel comfortable. Remember, the success of the decision-making model is reflected in the outcomes the committee produces, not the methods it uses.

COMMITTEE OUTCOMES

The congress's directive to the committee determines its final product. If the congress has asked your committee to distill a broad debate into an amendment, your product will be a clearly articulated, well-reasoned amendment that satisfies the concerns of all sides. You can use the information in Chapter 8 to create an amendment.

Committee Outcomes
• Amendment
• Resolution or Bill
• Report

If the congress requests the committee to develop a resolution or bill on a particular topic, the committee's goal will be to mold a document that clearly addresses the problem, taking into consideration the concerns of the congress as a whole. You can refer to Chapter 6 to help you develop a resolution.

Finally, the congress may ask your committee to produce a report. The outcome in this case is a clearly articulated report that addresses the congress's concerns. The report may be purely informational or it may provide the necessary information required for congress members to take action on the topic.

REPORTING TO THE ASSEMBLY

When a committee sends a resolution or amendment to the congress, the house considers it as soon as pending business is completed and before it takes up a new main motion, unless the congress's schedule allots time for committee reports. The committee's motion requires no second, since it is the work of more than one member of the assembly. All the rules for debating and voting on a regular motion apply to a committee motion. If the committee's proposal needs further refinement, the house can amend it or refer it back to the committee.

KEY CONCEPTS FROM CHAPTER 9

Benefits of Committees

Assemblies form committees to:

- Refine positions
- Gather information
- Prepare reports
- Develop positions

Forming Committees

When forming committees, the assembly considers the following:

- What is the committee's purpose?
- What results should be produced?
- Who will be on the committee? Why?
- How large should the committee be?

Decision Making in Committees

Decision making in committees is far more casual than it is in the main assembly.

- Committees frequently use two strategies to make decisions:
  - Standard Agenda Process
  - Nominal Group Technique

Committee Outcomes

The committee's final product depends on its mandate.

- Committees can produce
  - Reports
  - Amendments
  - Resolutions

Reporting to the Congress

- The congress considers a committee's amendment or resolution as soon as pending business is completed and before it takes up a new main motion, unless the schedule allots time for committee reports.

NOTES

1. Joann Keyton, *Communicating in Groups: Building Relationships for Effective Decision Making* (New York: Oxford University Press, 2002), p. 167.

2. Ibid., pp. 167–169.

3. Ibid., pp. 171–173.

Section 4

Conducting Competitive Congresses: Guidelines for Coaches, Judges, and Hosts

Chapter 10

Coaching: Preparing Students for Competitive Congress*

This chapter describes how to train students for competitive congresses. It first discusses how you can help your students prepare for these and then explains your responsibilities during the tournament. Finally, it describes how you can assist your students after the tournament is over. These guidelines should help you to become a competent coach and to create a cooperative and beneficial debating experience for you and your students.

HOW TO PREPARE DEBATERS BEFORE A TOURNAMENT

You can prepare your students for a legislative debate tournament in numerous ways: teaching them research skills, showing them how to develop their arguments; hosting practice rounds, and helping them improve their speaking styles. The coaching strategies explained in this section will not only help your students during student congresses but will also provide them with important tools that they can use in other areas of their lives.

Researching for Legislative Debate

In order to be successful, or even competitive, in legislative debate, a student must be knowledgeable of current events. More than many other forms of competitive public speaking, student congress revolves around political events. Students must have a deep enough understanding of these events to speak on multiple sides of the issues, often with little preparation during the assembly. As a coach, you must encourage your students to develop an

*Kari E. Wohlschlegel and Michael K. Middleton

awareness of current events. You can do so by requiring your students to follow a reading list. You should compile this list from an assortment of news sources: newspapers, journals, magazines, and books. Make sure your list includes various types of sources because each has different benefits. For example, newspaper articles provide up-to-date summaries of political events, while journal articles offer more in-depth analysis of political issues and problems. By having your students read different types of news sources, you can increase their political awareness.

Encourage your students to read a newspaper, either in print or electronic form, daily. These papers will provide students with the most current news and, when read regularly, will help students develop a more holistic view of politics and enable them to follow political trends.

You will often receive a list of the bills for discussion before an upcoming tournament. Make sure that your students prepare briefs on these and that all of your students have information on each topic. You can do this in several ways. First, you can require every student to research all the bills. This option ensures that each student has knowledge of every bill, and encourages students to research thoroughly because they cannot rely on the work of their teammates. Unfortunately, however, students cannot devote themselves entirely to legislative debate, and researching every bill thoroughly might present a time burden. As a result, they may have to gloss over some of the bills in order to gather evidence on all of them.

A second option is to divide the bills among team members and have them research only the bills they are given. They then exchange their research before the tournament. This option has two benefits. First, because the students are researching a smaller number of bills, they are likely to gather more sophisticated information on each. More extensive evidence on each bill will obviously help all the students during the congress. Second, sharing research encourages teamwork and cooperation. Since the students will have to share research, they will be forced to rely on each other for preparation. This option is especially beneficial for new teams whose members have had only limited experience in working together. Unfortunately, the cooperative aspect of this option also creates a problem. If a student does not do his or her share of the work, the other team members suffer. As the coach, you must decide which research option is appropriate. Feel free to try one option at one tournament and another one at a later event to see which works best for your team.

If you decide to use the second option, you should create a template for the research briefs. This will benefit the team because all members will be familiar with the template and so will access information quickly during the tournament. If you do not use the template, you run the risk of some students being unable to navigate a brief during the session. One of the easiest templates to use is to divide a paper in half vertically and list all the arguments for and against each bill. Number the arguments in each column with the sources included.

Developing Arguments for Legislative Debate

After the students have researched the topics, make sure that they prepare arguments for and against each bill. Remind them that they cannot ignore arguments with which they disagree; they must be able to address all sides of an issue. As a coach you must go beyond requiring students to formulate arguments for every issue. You must help them to fully develop and present these arguments effectively.

When evaluating a student's argument, don't just read it from the brief. Rather, have the student write and deliver a speech about the argument, similar to one he or she would give during a congress. Delivering a speech may be a challenge to some students who are more comfortable with presenting arguments in writing, but an oral presentation is important because arguments that sound good on paper may make little sense when spoken. Also, by requiring students to deliver an argument as a speech rather than merely "talking through" the argument, you force the student to state the argument in a clear, concise manner. This is important because students will have to learn to state their arguments quickly and clearly during the congress.

Remind your students that they can present effective arguments using a simple ARE format. This organization includes three important elements: assertion, reasoning, and evidence. The assertion is the claim of the argument, the reasoning is the analysis behind the argument, and the evidence is the facts that bolster the argument. For example:

Assertion: The United States should ratify the Kyoto Protocol.

Reasoning: International allies view the United States unfavorably because it refuses to ratify the treaty.

Evidence: Here, students should present evidence that supports their claim.

Obviously, your students should not say "assertion," "reasoning," and "evidence" during their speeches, but they should organize their speeches using this structure to make clear and effective arguments. Remind the students that they must fully explain their reasoning throughout their speeches.

Examine the evidence the students use for their arguments. Many topics require very recent evidence, so make sure that what they use is up to date. Also, check that students do not take their evidence out of context. They can easily alter the author's intent when citing only a few statistics or sentences from an article.

Your students should also include impacts in their arguments. Impacts are the overall point of an argument and ultimately give the audience a reason to care. A sample impact for the previously outlined argument would be, "If the United States does not ratify the Kyoto Protocol, it risks alienating allies who are key to a successful completion of the War on Terror." Be certain that your students include impacts because they are often the one part of an argument that the audience listens to, and students often win an argument on the impacts.

Listen closely for several elements while students deliver their speeches. First, make sure that the arguments make sense. Ask yourself several questions: Does the speech follow a logical order? Do you understand the arguments? Are the arguments well founded? The general impression you have of the speech is important because judges, especially those with little experience, will often weigh the speech based on their general impression of the arguments.

Pay attention to the rhetoric the students choose. Rhetoric is important because a well-crafted speech compels the judges and other competitors to listen to the speaker. Specifically, make sure your students use the active voice, which is more powerful than the passive. For example, "the spider bit her" (active voice) is clearer and more powerful than "she was bitten by the spider" (passive voice).

Encourage your students to use imagery whenever possible. Imagery, such as metaphors and similes, makes the speech more interesting and enhances the overall quality. The use of imagery also indicates to the judge that the speaker has devoted time to developing the speech, and the judge is likely to reward her for the effort. Also, suggest that your students incorporate tasteful jokes into their arguments to lighten the atmosphere and make your students stand out in the judge's mind. Judges always appreciate competitors who can make them laugh.

Make sure that your students do not use insensitive language. The most obvious form of this language is racial epithets, but you should also listen for gender normative rhetoric and generalizations about specific groups. Encourage your students to use more inclusive language, such as saying, "We should help the environment," as opposed to, "You should help the environment." Inclusive language creates a bond between the speaker and the audience. It signals that the speaker is not lecturing, but rather giving advice everyone should follow, and makes the speaker more likable to the judge.

To further help your students develop their argumentation skills, have them respond to their classmates' speeches either in a formal practice session or in a more informal setting. By having the students respond to one another, you force them to practice composing response speeches in a limited time. Just as important, you can determine whether they are adequately responding to arguments. Unfortunately, many students who are good at developing arguments are unable to quickly assess and debate other people's arguments. Make sure that the respondents are actually addressing the major points of the previous speakers and not avoiding the issues. Finally, make sure that your students continue to discuss relevant issues throughout the session, instead of repeating old arguments or debating tangential matters.

Although it may sound difficult and time consuming, evaluating arguments is actually quite easy. You simply need to apply the same logic you use in everyday life. Ultimately, if you follow the guidelines presented above and the argument makes sense to you, a judge is also likely to accept the student's arguments.

Holding Practice Sessions

Requiring your students to practice legislative debate is the most important thing you can do to help them prepare for a tournament. By practicing, they become comfortable speaking in front of an audience and following the assembly's rules of order. Practice rounds can either be held on a team or individual level, and you will probably want to try both. Team practices are beneficial when students want to become familiar with parliamentary rules, while individual practices are useful when you wish to focus on speaking styles and effectiveness.

Holding a practice legislative session is best when the majority of the team can participate, because it can more closely mimic an actual congress. You may even want to hold a joint practice session with other schools. This not only fosters a feeling of camaraderie between the schools, which will make the congress more pleasant, but also creates a better practicing environment because it includes people who may have different points of view on the topics.

To hold a team or a joint-team practice, simply gather the students into a room large enough to hold everyone. Although you do not need to use the formal seating arrangements that occur in a student congress, you should require your students to act as if they were in an actual legislative debate and to follow all the rules of order. Listen to the students' speeches and take notes on both the positive and negative aspects of their presentations. You can then critique the speeches in one of two ways: have everyone pause after a speech so that you can give the speaker your comments, or save your analysis until the end of the session. Although the first option may disrupt the flow of the argumentation, it allows you to deliver a comprehensive critique to each student when the speech is fresh in his or her mind. However, the second option makes the practice round more realistic and allows you to critique the development of arguments. It is also less time consuming. Decide which method to use based on your time constraints and what you hope to accomplish.

Individual practice sessions are also important tools in creating competitive public speakers. These practices are beneficial because they enable you to focus exclusively on one student, so you can give a more in-depth critique of her speeches. To hold an individual practice, ask the student to deliver either one or multiple speeches (depending on how long you want the practice to last). As with team practice, you can critique the performance in two ways. One is to stop the speech every time your student makes a mistake and tell her what she did wrong. This option gives the speaker a chance to improve during the rest of the speech, but it can be frustrating, especially if the speaker is new to legislative debate and is making multiple mistakes. You can also have the student complete the speech before you offer your evaluation. This method allows for a more realistic experience, since the judge is unlikely to stop speakers in the middle of their speeches. However, because the speaker does not have the opportunity to overcome problems during the speech, she may have to repeat the speech to correct mistakes.

Training Better Speakers

While hosting the practice session, pay attention not only to the students' arguments but also to their speaking styles. "Speaking style" refers to elements such as the speaker's fluency, pitch and speed variations, and gestures. Improving your students speaking styles is essential for creating successful debaters, because speaking style is often the most noticeable aspect of public speaking.

Fluency is important because it portrays confidence and knowledge. When students are prepared to speak on a topic and they are well briefed on the relevant issues, their speaking is likely to be fluent. Thus, judges are likely to reward those students who are fluent because they have dedicated more time to preparation. Furthermore, a fluent speaker is much more enjoyable than one who has frequent vocal pauses. If your students lack fluency, they are likely to alienate the judges and thus not score well.

Lack of fluency commonly arises from several causes. Inexperienced debaters will have problems because of their fear of public speaking. They probably will become easily flustered and stop several times in the middle of their speeches. This is completely normal. Speaking in front of an audience, especially one composed of your peers, can be a frightening experience. The best way to help these students is to emphasize the importance of practice. Frequent practice is really the only way to overcome initial fluency problems. Encourage them to practice on their own, in front of their family or even a mirror. Another reason even experienced debaters have problems with fluency is that they do not know much about a topic, so obviously you should tell these students to research further.

Lack of fluency also arises from an inability to quickly develop arguments from the research materials gathered and to articulate a message with minimal rehearsal. You can hold a few drills to help your students overcome these problems. To help a student think on his feet, have him speak without preparation on a series of topics from the research the team or the debater is preparing. For example, you may ask him to give an impromptu speech on the environment. After the student has talked about the environment for a short time (anywhere between 15 seconds to a minute), shout out a new topic, such as the International Criminal Court.

The student must immediately transition to that topic. Keep changing topics until the student has a fluency break (a vocal pause). You can hold this drill with only one student, or you can set it up as a competition to see which student can speak the longest without a fluency break.

For students who slur their speech or have difficulty articulating clearly without extensive rehearsal, you can hold a drill involving tongue twisters. Simply ask the students to say tongue twisters aloud. This drill is especially beneficial just before a legislative debate because it warms up the debaters' vocal chords. Collect a variety of tongue twisters and distribute them to your team. You can find numerous tongue twisters online and in books. For example, the 1st International Collection of Tongue Twisters, available at http://www.uebersetzung.at/twister, offers a variety of examples in several languages.

You also need to examine your students' pitch and speed variation. Good public speakers change their pitch and speed to keep the audience involved. For example, when quoting other speakers, participants should use a lower pitch to draw attention to the quoted material. This change in pitch helps the audience distinguish the speaker's argument from the argument in the quote. Changing pitch makes it easier for the audience to follow arguments and will improve the judges' response.

Speakers should also vary their speed for emphasis. For example, a debater should speak slowly when discussing crucial points to ensure that the audience is listening. Changes in speed will keep the audience involved, and thus the judge is likely to respond more positively to the speaker. There are no simple drills or tips on how to improve your students' pitch and speed variations, so you must pay attention to these during practice and be sure to comment on them during your critique.

Gestures are another important element of speaking style. They can significantly add to a speech by capturing the attention of the audience and emphasizing important points, or they can hurt a speech by becoming a distraction. Unfortunately, students who are new to competitive public speaking often have a very difficult time perfecting their gestures. Usually, inexperienced public speakers will either have excessive, nervous gestures or none at all. Both of these styles detract from the quality of a speech. To help your students develop good gestures, have them identify approximately five gestures that they feel comfortable with and that you think will be beneficial to a speech. Have them incorporate those gestures in all of their speeches, until the gestures feel natural. After they have mastered these, have them add a few more to their repertoire. Mastering gestures is important because good use of gestures can be the difference between a winning or losing speech.

COACHING DURING A COMPETITIVE STUDENT CONGRESS

A competitive student congress has the potential of an enjoyable, rewarding experience for both coaches and students. Unfortunately, it can also be very stressful for both parties. As a coach, you should make the tournament the most relaxed experience possible. You can adopt several strategies to achieve this.

Interact with your students as much as possible. A high level of interaction opens lines of communication and helps you to form a more cohesive relationship with your team. During recesses and after tournaments, talk to your students about how it went and how they think they did. The feedback you receive, such as items they wish to work on, can be helpful in future practice. If they are discouraged, as many inexperienced students are when they are not as successful as experienced speakers, try to bolster their confidence and assure them that debating gets easier with time and practice. Overall, try to help them have an enjoyable time, because they will learn more if they enjoy the event.

Some tournaments will have a tab room that is open to the coaches and sponsors so you can watch the officials tabulate the results. Although it may be tempting, you should try to avoid entering the tab room. Especially at large tournaments, the officials have to concentrate on tabulating numerous results, and frequent interruptions increase the likelihood of miscalculations.

Remind your students to practice proper tournament etiquette. Explain to them that student congress is not only a forum for discussing ideas but also an activity through which they build relationships. Encourage your students to get to know competitors, be polite, and always be supportive of their peers. Similarly, emphasize that they be respectful and courteous toward judges and tournament officials. If, after a tournament, they feel a judge rated them unfairly, have them consider why the judge rated them as she did or suggest that they approach the judge at another tournament and ask advice about how to improve. By encouraging this etiquette, you will ensure that students gain more than competitive success from a tournament.

Coaching after a Congress

Your job as coach continues after an event is over, as you help your students improve their legislative debate skills. Review the scores of all of your competitors to get an idea of their personal strengths and weaknesses. Ask the students who consistently received low scores if they know what they did wrong, and make a list of what they should work on during the next practice session. Then, identify the students who improved their scores and find out what they think was behind the improvement. You obviously should continue with those drills they found useful, and try to develop new ones that will help them perform even better. Finally, talk to the rest of your students about what they think they must work on to improve their performances. Be sure to implement these ideas during the next practice sessions.

Many debaters blame the judge for their poor scores, either because they do not want to admit they did not perform well, or because they do not realize the mistakes they made. Encourage your students not to scapegoat the judge. Point out that the judge's reaction to the debate is a legitimate perspective that they should try to understand and better accommodate. Then, ask your students how they could have better adapted to the judge in order to receive high scores. Ultimately, adapting to the judge is the key to success in legislative debate and teaches an important lesson about advocacy in other areas of students' lives.

Holding individual evaluation sessions immediately after a congress is extremely important. These discussions allow you to tailor your critique to the specific needs of the individual students and to present your comments while the event is still fresh in their minds. Often students perform differently in a tournament than in a practice round because of the pressure, and so the criticism you give them on a practice speech may not be applicable to their tournament performance.

Also, talk to your students as a group. Ask them to evaluate the event and suggest what they might want to change. This step is especially important for new teams whose members may not be comfortable interacting with each other. It also makes future events more enjoyable.

Ultimately, coaching is not difficult as long as you understand the basic strategies and techniques outlined in this chapter. Despite the intensive effort these tasks require, watching students develop from novice speakers to experienced advocates provides a great deal of reward.

KEY CONCEPTS FROM CHAPTER 10

Before the Tournament

- Encourage the students to research.
- Help students prepare arguments.
- Aid students in improving their rhetoric.
- Host practice rounds.
- Lead fluency drills.
- Encourage pitch and speed variations.
- Practice gestures.

During the Tournament

- Interact with your students.
- Try to avoid entering the tabulation room often.

After the Tournament

- Review the scores your team has received.
- Talk to students individually about their experiences.
- Get feedback from the team as a whole.

Chapter 11
Evaluating Debate: Judging in Competitive Student Congresses*

This chapter examines the role of judges in legislative debate. It first explains the basic procedural duties of judges—such as keeping time and scoring speeches—and then describes what a judge should look for when scoring speeches. With these resources, you should be well prepared to undertake one of the most important tasks in running a competitive congress.

JUDGING RESPONSIBILITIES

The basic steps that you must take as a judge during each legislative debate are fairly simple, although the specific procedures may vary from tournament to tournament. When you follow these correctly, you ensure that the session will move smoothly.[1]

Before the congress begins, the host will provide you with a chart of where each participant is seating. Once you are in the session, the interim presiding officer, usually the host, calls roll to ensure that everyone is present and seated as the chart indicates. Next, the congress will elect a chair, or presiding officer, through the process described in Section 2. Once the roll and elections are completed, the tournament begins. Some organizations, such as the U.S. National Forensic League (NFL), require that sessions last a certain number of hours. If you are judging a tournament that has this rule, be sure to note the time that the session begins and ends.

*Kari E. Wohlschlegel and Michael K. Middleton

Timing

As the judge (though more commonly you will be referred to as the official scorer), one of your primary duties is to time the speakers. No speech may exceed three minutes, though the chairperson can allow the speaker to finish his or her sentence at the expiration of three minutes. The house, however, may yield the speaker more time by suspending the rules or through the use of some other parliamentary procedure. The speaker may also answer a question in overtime, but the response should not exceed 30 seconds. Longer speeches are allowed only if the tournament director stipulates such an exception. Bear in mind that parliamentary motions and questions are not counted as speeches.

You can keep time in numerous ways. The simplest is to say, "Time" at the end of three minutes. However, because this does not give the speaker an indication of time remaining as she speaks, timekeepers generally use time cards (which the host often provides). These time cards should have "2 minutes," "1 minute," and "30 seconds" written on them. At the expiration of one minute, hold up the "2 minute" card so that the speaker and other assembly members can see it. When only one minute remains, hold up the "1 minute" card. Finally, when 30 seconds remain, show the "30 second" card. At the end of three minutes, say "Time," and allow the speaker to finish, if necessary.

If you have not received time cards, or do not want to use them, you may use a bell to keep time. Ring it once at the expiration of two minutes. Then, after three minutes, ring it twice to indicate time has expired. Again, allow the speaker limited time to finish her sentence, or to respond to a question.

Scoring

Your most important task as a judge is scoring the speeches. It is essential to a competitive congress because it determines the superior participants in each tournament. The method of scoring depends on the tabulation system the tournament director establishes, and the tournament officials must provide you with specific instructions. However, the basic procedure for scoring is the same regardless of the tab system.

Because some congresses involve numerous participants, you may have difficulty identifying and remembering the speakers. To help you remember, place a coin on your seating chart over the name of the person speaking so you can avoid scoring errors.

Once a speaker finishes her speech, you must award points on a scale of one to six. The best speeches receive six points, while the worst earn one point. Whatever score you assign, you must record it on the official scoring sheet or seating chart, if the officials did not provide a separate scoring sheet.

Below is a ballot that you may use to guide your judging and to provide consistent standards for evaluation. This ballot includes the major criteria against which you should evaluate a speech. By scoring each category and then averaging the scores, you standardize your scoring. You do not have to use this ballot. Ultimately, your opinion is correct as long as you can justify your decision, if called on. The reasons underlying your decision provide the feedback you can share with competitors who approach you seeking to improve their performance.

Finally, at the end of each hour of her tenure, you award the presiding officer between one and six points depending on how well she has fulfilled her duties. Because presiding officers are not permitted to speak in the debates, this practice ensures that they are not unfairly disadvantaged in the competition for points. In the case of the presiding officer, hourly evaluation is comparable to evaluating a delegate's multiple speeches. If the congress has formed committees and the tournament wishes to score such activities (this decision can be made on a case-by-case basis and in consultation with any league rules governing your tournament), then participation on a committee counts as one speech. Each committee member receives a score from one to six based on the contribution of the committee and the quality of the committee's report, resolution, amendment, or other results. The committee spokesperson does not receive additional points for presenting the report, because the report represents the views of the entire committee.

Optional Student Congress Ballot*

Verbal Elements

Fluency—Does the speaker stumble on their words excessively?

Poor 1   2   3   4   5   6 Excellent

Vocal Variety—Is the speaker monotone or do they use their voice effectively?

Poor 1   2   3   4   5   6 Excellent

Clear Imagery—Does the speaker make the issue clearly understandable, i.e., does the speaker "paint a picture" for the audience?

Poor 1   2   3   4   5   6 Excellent

Word Choice—Does the speaker use effective word choices, rhetorical devices, etc.?

Poor 1   2   3   4   5   6 Excellent

Humor—Does the speaker attempt to use humor? Is it in good taste?

Poor 1   2   3   4   5   6 Excellent

Effective Language—Does the speaker use active, forceful, direct language or is he or she ambiguous, passive, timid?

Poor 1   2   3   4   5   6 Excellent

Appropriateness—Does the speaker attack any group or person? Does the speaker foster an open environment?

Poor 1   2   3   4   5   6 Excellent

Nonverbal Elements

Use of Notes—Does the speaker use notes in a limited fashion?

Poor 1   2   3   4   5   6 Excellent

Eye Contact—Does the speaker use effective eye contact with the entire audience?

Poor 1   2   3   4   5   6 Excellent

Nonverbal Elements (*continued*)

Gestures—Does the speaker use effective gestures or distracting ones?

Poor 1   2   3   4   5   6 Excellent

Posture & Demeanor—Is the speaker confident, forceful, inviting?

Poor 1   2   3   4   5   6 Excellent

Argument Elements

Organization—Does the speech "make sense" as you listen to it?

Poor 1   2   3   4   5   6 Excellent

Relevance—Are the arguments relevant to the direction in which the debate is moving?

Poor 1   2   3   4   5   6 Excellent

Responsive—Does it address the topics under discussion directly?

Poor 1   2   3   4   5   6 Excellent

Internally Sound—Are assertions properly supported?

Poor 1   2   3   4   5   6 Excellent

Use of Evidence—Does the speaker responsibly use quality evidence?

Poor 1   2   3   4   5   6 Excellent

Sound Logic—Does the speaker rely on spurious relationships to warrant claims?

Poor 1   2   3   4   5   6 Excellent

Quality of Implications—Does the speaker answer the "so what?" question?

Poor 1   2   3   4   5   6 Excellent

TOTAL SCORE:

*Use this ballot as a guide or fill it out and average the individual scores to determine an individual's average on a speech.

What to Judge

Determining how many points to award to a speech can be a difficult process. Novice judges may find it hard to distinguish between a speech that deserves four points and one that deserves five. Nevertheless, analyzing several key factors will help you judge the overall quality of the speech. These factors include the validity and quality of the speaker's arguments as well as important verbal and nonverbal elements. (Many of these are included on the ballot above.) You should examine each of these factors independently to determine the overall quality of the speech.

Argument

Effective argumentation is essential for any speaker in legislative debate, and so it is obviously an important factor on which you must focus. You may find it difficult to adequately assess the validity and value of an argument, especially when it is dealing with an emotionally charged topic, but there are specific elements of an argument you can examine to make a holistic and unbiased judgment. Five important elements of effective argumentation are:

- Organization
- Arguments: Relevance, Responsiveness, Internal Structure
- Use of Evidence
- Causality
- Impact

Evaluate Organization

Score the organization of the speech. To do this, ask yourself questions, such as these:

- Do the arguments follow a logical sequence?
- Is the argument clear and concise?

Organization is critical to effective argumentation because it ensures that the speakers present their arguments clearly. When judging organization, note whether the speaker has presented a preview of the major points she will make in the body of the speech. This preview gives you and the audience a clear understanding of the direction of the argument. Another indicator of good organization is how well the speaker stays within the time parameters. Speakers that go significantly under time or over time are usually not well organized and prepared. Also, if the speaker spends a significant amount of time describing the first major point but very little on the others, it is likely he was not organized.[2] Ultimately, a speech that lacks organization will also lose effectiveness because the speaker has not explored important questions related to an issue. Thus, you should penalize those speeches that seem to ramble and lack direction.

Evaluate Arguments

You must evaluate the arguments presented. As a novice judge, you may find this task daunting, but remember that most people evaluate arguments all the time, whether it be the arguments of your colleagues or of politicians. To evaluate an argument in a student congress, you go through the same steps you would in your daily life.

1. **Determine whether the speaker's arguments are relevant to the current discussion.**[3] During legislative sessions, debates often evolve and focus on different issues. Make sure that the speaker has followed this movement and is addressing the current discussion, rather than talking about topics already covered adequately.

2. **Make sure the arguments are responsive to the previous speeches.** Even if the speaker is talking about the current topic, he or she may be skirting the issue rather than responding effectively.[4] Consider this example in a debate on recycling: The first speaker argues that more recycling would improve the quality of the environment. The second speaker responds that spending on the environment has increased over the past five years. While the second speaker is dealing with the relevant issue being debated, she has failed to respond to the first speaker's argument. Increased spending has little to do with whether or not recycling will improve our environment and, therefore, is not responsive to the claim that more recycling is needed. As a judge, you should penalize the speakers who do not respond directly to the previous speeches, because they are not properly engaging the arguments in the session.

3. **Examine the internal structure of each argument.** For an argument to be effective and persuasive, it should have three important

elements: assertion (A), reasoning (R), and evidence (E). The assertion is the claim of the argument, reasoning is the warrant behind the argument, and evidence is the analysis backing up the argument.[5] The ARE format provides the listener with a clear, logical argument. The following is an example of the format:

> **Assertion:** The United Nations should intervene in Darfur.
>
> **Reasoning:** Genocide is occurring within Darfur.
>
> **Evidence:** Numerous UN treaties obligate member countries to intervene to stop genocide.

Make sure a speaker's argument includes these three important elements. The speaker will not say "assertion," etc, during his speech; however, if you listen carefully, you can identify these elements in properly constructed arguments. Reward the speakers who use this argumentation format, because they are likely to have a more persuasive speech.

4. **Examine the speaker's use of evidence.** The speaker's evidence should be current, especially on topics that change quickly. Using current evidence ensures that participants are debating the most relevant and up-to-date issues, so reward the speakers who do this. Speakers must also present their evidence in an unbiased way. They can warp the intent of an author and take an expert's words out of context. Monitor this, and deduct points from the speakers who misuse the evidence.

5. **Scrutinize the speaker's idea of causality.** Debaters often use causal relationships to make arguments and provide important implications. Unfortunately, they can easily stretch these relationships much further than they should go.[6] Here is an example: a speaker is talking about the ramifications of the United States condemning Russian activities in Chechnya. This speaker argues that if the United States condemns Russian activities, Russia will likely respond with a condemnation. The speaker explains that this situation is likely to continue, with the US–Russian relationship slowly deteriorating until they revert to Cold War relations. The speaker then predicts that these Cold War relations could lead to nuclear war. Thus, US condemnation of Russian activities would cause a nuclear war. Obviously, this speaker has exaggerated the effect of this hypothetical scenario. Pay attention to

the speaker's use of causal relationships to ensure that she has presented a sound argument as opposed to one based on spurious relationships.

6. **Evaluate the implications of the arguments presented.** The implications of an argument are important because they provide the audience with a reason to care. In other words, they answer the important "so what?" question. Often, speakers make arguments without providing the overall implications. For example, a speaker may argue that if countries do not place stronger restrictions on the burning of fossil fuels by corporations, global warming will continue at an alarming rate. The implications of this argument are the ramifications of global warming—changing climate patterns that cause devastating natural disasters, and melting ice caps that threaten massive flooding. Award points to those speakers who clearly state the implications of their argument.

Ultimately, when judging arguments, you just use simple logic. Listen closely to the speakers to ensure that they present a clearly organized proposition that is supported by solid reasoning and evidence. In the end, rank well those speakers who are successful in persuading *you*. They likely fulfilled most of these important elements of communication.

Verbal Elements

Numerous verbal elements affect the quality of the speech. These are important, and so you must include them in your overall evaluation. Focus on seven key elements as you assess the speech:

- Fluency
- Vocal Presentation, i.e., pitch, rate, vocal variety
- Vocabulary
- Clarity
- Humor
- Word Economy
- Biased Language

Fluency

Fluency is an essential trait for all good speakers, because it entices the audience to listen attentively. If a speech is broken up by numerous vocal pauses or filler words, such as, "um . . .," the audience quickly loses patience. Fluency also indicates how much effort the speaker has put into preparation. Often, speakers improve their fluency with practice, and so a very fluent speech would indicate that the speaker has devoted a lot of time to preparation. In addition, speakers who are knowledgeable about and comfortable with their subject usually speak more fluently. Thus, fluency is an indication of how much research speakers have done. However, when judging a speaker's fluency, you must take into account that some debaters may be speaking in a second language.

Vocal Presentation

The speed, the pitch, and the variation of the person's speaking pattern often determine the overall success of the speech. If the speaker were to speak in a monotone and use only one speed for the entire speech, you would likely become bored rapidly and stop listening. Thus, while listening to a speaker, ask yourself: "Does he change pitch often?"; "Does she alter her speed depending on the importance of points?"; "Is the speaking pattern effective and does it hold my interest?" By answering these questions, you can better judge the quality of the speaker's verbal elements. These elements not only make the speech more pleasing but also indicate the amount of time and effort the speaker put into preparation.

Vocabulary

Examine the vocabulary and rhetorical devices a speaker uses. Utilizing direct language and vivid rhetorical devices keeps the audience actively engaged. And most likely, speakers who employ very imaginative words and use rhetorical devices such as metaphors and similes have taken a significant amount of time preparing their speeches.[7] A debater should receive credit for the time spent making the speech interesting and accessible.

Check that the speaker is using the active voice; it is stronger than the passive in presenting an argument.[8] An example of passive voice is "He was rebuked by his teacher." An example of active voice is "The teacher rebuked him." The latter is obviously a much stronger sentence, and you should reward speakers who use the active voice. However, do not penalize participants for quoting material that uses the passive.

Clarity

The primary goal of all speakers is to be understood. Thus, you should reward those debaters who speak clearly and effectively. Speakers who use complex words or jargon may sound intelligent, but if the audience does not understand their message, they have failed in their primary objective. You should penalize those speakers who rely heavily on jargon and overly complicated rhetoric, because this impairs the overall effectiveness of their speech.

Humor

Humor will help maintain the interest of the audience during a long legislative session, which can last anywhere between five and eight hours. Unfortunately, many students are not as successful at delivering humor as some may expect. Thus, do not penalize a speaker for not including humor or lacking perfect comedic timing. You should, however, reward those who dedicate the time to develop a joke and those who attempt to use humor. Remember that speakers should use humor only as an embellishment, not as the dominating element in their speeches. Student congresses discuss important matters, so the humor should not eclipse the issues.

Word Economy

Pay attention to the speaker's word economy. Often, when speakers become nervous or are not knowledgeable about the topic, they begin to ramble or use unnecessary "filler" words, such as "We can see that." These provide no substance to the speech, and speakers often use them when unsure of what to say next. Also, penalize speakers who use language that makes them sound weak or tentative, such as "I believe" or "I think." These words indicate that the speaker is not an expert on the subject and thus should not be trusted. If the speaker says, "I think we must sign the Kyoto Protocol to save the environment," his message would not be as strong as if he were to say, "We must sign the Kyoto Protocol to save the environment." The latter is more persuasive because it emphasizes an action rather than an opinion. Therefore, reward speakers who use stronger, more persuasive rhetoric and penalize those who show a lack of confidence in the words they choose.

Biased Language
Severely penalize any speaker who makes personal attacks or uses biased language. Student congresses are meant to foster cooperation and discussion; they must not be used as a forum to assault other students. Listen carefully to ensure that speakers are not belittling or verbally assaulting any individual or group. You will rarely encounter blatant bias, but you should watch for less obvious forms of inappropriate language. One of the most common examples of biased language is male-normative language. For example, a student who refers to law enforcement officers as policemen, instead of police officers, is using biased language. Reward speakers who avoid such missteps and seek to be inclusive; they help the congress fulfill its role as a cooperative form of debate.

NONVERBAL ELEMENTS
Nonverbal elements are as important to the effectiveness of a speech as verbal elements, and so, as judge, you should give them equal weight. The nonverbal elements of a speech improve its overall quality by portraying the speaker as confident and in control. Four of the most important are

+ Use of Notes
+ Eye Contact
+ Use and Variety of Gestures
+ Posture

Use of Notes
Legislative debate does not require speakers to memorize their speeches, but participants should not rely heavily on notes. Excessive reading from notes distracts the audience, and the speaker loses persuasiveness. Furthermore, reliance on notes indicates that the speaker is unprepared and uncomfortable with the topic. A strong speaker should use notes sparingly, only for prompting or direction.

Eye Contact
Many people, particularly those new to public speaking, find sustaining eye contact with the audience difficult, but it is an important element in debate because it shows that the speaker is confident. Furthermore, eye

contact creates a connection between audience members and the speaker that encourages the audience to listen actively.[9] You should reward eye contact because it demonstrates the speaker's strength.

Use and Variety of Gestures

Public speakers must appear confident, and using gestures is a good way to show this. Unfortunately, speakers often use gestures poorly, with the result that they look tense and flustered. Make sure that a speaker's gestures are adding to, rather than hurting, the presentation.

One of the most common types of inappropriate gestures is known as adaptors—unintentional body movements that relieve stress or reduce boredom. Common adaptors are tapping a pencil, swaying back and forth, or chewing gum. These gestures distract the audience and signal that a speaker is uncomfortable. Speakers can overcome these gestures through practice and experience, and so, you should penalize a speaker for excessive adaptors.[10]

Deliberate bodily movements can enhance the content of a speech. These gestures visually reinforce the speaker's message. For example, when you make wide gestures with your arms, you are reinforcing the idea that something is large. These types of gestures also keep the audience engaged by drawing attention to the speaker. However, excessive use of gestures can become distracting. Reward the speakers who use effective and varied gestures that enhance the message of their speech.

Posture

Scholars in communication have noted that audiences focus on a limited number of characteristics when assessing a public speaker. Good posture is one of the most important. Speakers who demonstrate good posture are relaxed, smile, and emit an aura of confidence and intelligence. Audiences want to listen to them because they appear knowledgeable.

Speakers who have poor posture are likely to face many problems. First, poor posture makes it more difficult to breathe deeply, and so, the speaker will not be able to talk forcefully. Furthermore, speakers with poor posture look uncomfortable, and as a result, an audience is less likely to respond positively to their speeches. As a judge, you should score the posture of the speaker, examining whether he is hunched over or standing straight.

Note how often the speaker smiles. A smile is an important tool for all public speakers, because audiences who see a presenter smiling are likely to think her engaging and friendly and will respond in kind. Bear in mind, however, that smiling is not always appropriate. Obviously, if the speaker is discussing the millions who have died from AIDS, or the horrors of the genocide in Darfur, a smile would be inappropriate.

Judging Responsibilities

- One of a judge's duties is to time the speakers.
- The judge's principal duty is to score the speeches.

What to Judge

- Argument Elements

  - Organization: Does the speech "make sense" as you listen to it?
  - Relevance: Are the arguments relevant to the direction in which the debate is moving?
  - Responsive: Does it address the topics under discussion directly?
  - Internal Structure: Are assertions properly supported?
  - Use of Evidence: Does the speaker responsibly use quality evidence?
  - Causality: Does the speaker rely on spurious relationships to warrant claims?
  - Quality of Implications: Does the speaker answer the "so what?" question?

- Verbal Elements

  - Fluency: Does the speaker stumble on his words excessively?
  - Vocal Presentation: Is the speaker monotone or does she use her voice effectively?
  - Vocabulary: Does the speaker make the issue clearly understandable, i.e., does the speaker "paint a picture" for the audience?
  - Clarity: Does the speaker use effective word choices, rhetorical devices, etc.?
  - Humor: Does the speaker attempt to use humor? Is it in good taste?

(continues)

- Word Economy: Does the speaker use active, forceful, direct language or is he or she ambiguous, passive, timid?
- Biased Language: Does the speaker attack any group or person? Does the speaker foster an open environment?
- Nonverbal Elements
  - Use of Notes: Does the speaker use notes in a limited fashion?
  - Eye Contact: Does the speaker use effective eye contact with the entire audience?
  - Gestures: Does the speaker use effective gestures or distracting ones?
  - Posture & Demeanor: Is the speaker confident, forceful, inviting?

NOTES

1. As adapted from the National Forensic League's Student Congress Manual, available at http://www.nflonline.org/uploads/DistrictInformation/conman.pdf .

2. Alfred Snider and Maxwell Schnurer, *Many Sides: Debate across the Curriculum* (New York: International Debate Education Association, 2002), p. 153.

3. Ibid., p. 155.

4. Ibid.

5. Ibid., p. 156.

6. Ibid.

7. Patricia Kearny and Timothy G. Plax, *Public Speaking in a Diverse Society* (Stamford, CT: Thomson, 2004), p. 252.

8. Ibid., p. 253.

9. Snider and Schnurer, p. 153.

10. Kearny and Plax, p. 267.

Chapter 12

Hosting: Preparing Your Competitive Congress*

As a host or director of a student congress, you have responsibilities before, during, and after the tournament. Each congress will present unique challenges based on resources, support, and interest. However, this chapter will give you the basic tools necessary to provide a positive educational experience for all participants. If you begin planning early and follow the guidelines below, preparation will proceed smoothly. Because the tasks discussed are interconnected, review the entire chapter thoroughly before you begin preparing.

PREPARATIONS BEFORE THE TOURNAMENT

As host, your work begins well before the tournament starts. You have to determine the location and time of your assembly, acquire the necessary materials, secure a reliable staff, and solicit participants. While these tasks may seem mundane, the decisions you make in the planning stage will determine the success of your tournament.

Time and Location

Your first step is planning when and where to hold your congress. To maximize participation, hold it when no other forensic activities are scheduled in your area. If you are hosting in an area where student congress is already part of a competitive forensics organization, e.g., NFL member schools, you can obtain schedules from participating schools indicating what days—usually weekends—are open. If this type of tournament is

---

*Kari E. Wohlschlegel and Michael K. Middleton

new to your area, make sure that your date does not conflict with events that would attract the same participants.

Make sure that you choose suitable facilities. Congresses can be as small as 20 to 30 participants or as large as over 100 members. If your school is too small, consider asking community groups with large meeting space, e.g., rotary club, city hall, YMCA, etc., to provide the facilities, or you can split the assembly and have multiple concurrent sessions.

When determining if a space is suitable, consider three things:

1. Make sure that the room you choose has enough space for everyone to work comfortably. Because participants often take notes and prepare speeches during the session, the assembly chamber should have work surfaces for the students.

2. Make sure that the parliamentarian, judge, and presiding officer have a clear line of sight to the assembly-at-large and vice versa. The chair must be able to see the participants so that she can recognize students in a fair manner and manage the proceedings efficiently. Many first-time hosts assume that using a classroom is preferable to using an auditorium because it provides a work surface for each participant. Unfortunately, because all participants are on the same level, this arrangement often results in the chair overlooking students or being unable to control disruptive members.

   Your best option is a lecture room with an elevated stage large enough for the chair, judge, parliamentarian, and a speaking platform. This setting maximizes visibility and ensures that speakers will receive full attention, because they will be addressing the assembly from the central podium rather than from various corners of a room that might not have suitable acoustics. A lecture room also provides the desks competitors need to work effectively. If your school does not have such a space, ask a local college if you can use its facilities.

3. Make sure that the facilities are available not only for the date but also for the amount of time required plus two to three hours before and after to set up before and clean up afterward. A student congress usually takes at least eight hours, not counting set-up and clean-up.

Invitation

Once you have fixed the date and location of your tournament, you need to prepare your invitation. Potential participants should receive it at least a month in advance of the event to ensure a good response. Don't wait until you have prepared all the tournament materials before you send it out.

Your invitation should include the following:

1. **Date and time.** Remember to follow the procedure discussed above and then double-check the date. Inaccurate or frequently changing information will discourage participation.

2. **Eligibility.** In areas where forensics competition is popular, you may wish to invite only members of school teams. Alternatively, you may open the tournament to all students in a certain age group. You should also consider level of experience when determining eligibility. If you are trying to build interest in student congress, you may wish to indicate that only individuals with no prior experience, less than one year, etc., are eligible. Alternately, you may want to stage a highly competitive tournament and create eligibility requirements accordingly. If you have ample space and resources, you may want to host two concurrent sessions. In that case, you should reserve one session for inexperienced participants and the other for more experienced competitors.

   If you want your tournament to appeal to the widest range of competitors possible, announce that it will have special recognition for inexperienced competitors. If you choose this approach, have participants indicate their experience level prior to the event so your tabulation staff can easily track their performance.

3. **Deadlines and Entry Caps.** Make sure to include an entry deadline, for example, 10 days before your tournament. You may also want to establish a deadline (for example, 48 hours) after which participants may not withdraw without a small penalty—no more than $10 to $15. Coupling this with an entry bond refundable upon arrival will probably offer the necessary incentive to prevent participants from dropping out without sufficient notice. Additionally, if you are allowing organizations or schools to enter their teams, you should indicate an entry cap per school. For example, you may permit no more than four competitors from each school. This maximizes the number of

schools that can participate by preventing one school from flooding the tournament.

4. **Tabulation Process.** Announce the tabulation process you will be using after careful consideration of which is appropriate (see Chapter 13). Your invitation is your commitment to participants, so you cannot change the process once you announce it.

5. **Provisions for Judging.** Indicate whether you will use a panel of judges or a single judge. If you are using community members as judges, announce the special persons or VIPs who will be fulfilling this function. You may also use your invitation to solicit judges. You can ask schools to bring a certain number of judges, for example, one judge for every four competitors, or more informally, ask the schools to contact you if they can provide judges.

6. **Procedure for Creating the Legislation Packet.** Indicate whether you will accept submissions for a packet (and if so, the deadline for submissions), when you will distribute the packet, and whether the agenda is open or closed (see below). If you are not setting the agenda but want members to arrive with their own topics and legislative items, announce this and provide necessary guidelines.

7. **Additional Information.** Make sure to include contact information and provide any additional information that may help your invitees decide whether they want to participate. For example, you might want to include a tentative schedule for the session or mention how many participants will receive awards at the tournament's end. And if participants are coming from out of town, include information about accommodations.

8. **Fees.** You will need to consider whether to charge fees for participating. In the United States, competitive forensics events customarily charge each participant a small fee to cover facilities and materials costs. If you decide to charge fees, keep them as low as possible, particularly if student congress is a new event and you are trying to build interest. Four to six dollars per participant is reasonable. Some tournaments also include a school or organization fee of $10 to $15 in addition to a participant fee. So, for example, if you charged minimum fees and Green Lawn High School brought four competitors, it would pay $26: $10 for the school and $4 for each of its four competitors.

Materials

One of the host's most overwhelming responsibilities is gathering the necessary materials to run a tournament successfully. These include the legislation packet, tabulation materials, and assembly members and judges materials.

Legislation Packet

You must determine how you will handle the tournament's legislative agenda early in your preparation, because you need to announce this in the invitation. You have several options:

1. **Have no formal legislation packet.** Instead of supplying a packet, announce that deliberations are open to items that the participants bring to the congress. You can ask the delegates to bring a certain number of items and allow the session to develop as members see fit. If you choose this option, provide guidelines on the form members should use in introducing bills and resolutions. The samples in the appendixes provide examples of these. In addition to easing your workload, this approach places a heavier focus on the competitors' preparation, since they will face an unpredictable agenda. This option works best when hosting a session for experienced debaters.

2. **Solicit bills and resolutions from participants.** Compile the submissions and distribute them before the event. Many tournaments prefer this approach because it eases the workload of organizers while enabling students to do detailed research and thus be better prepared to participate in debate. This is an especially good strategy if you are trying to attract new participants, who may be apprehensive about impromptu discussion.

3. **Develop the agenda yourself.** If the response to your solicitation is minimal or lacks variety, you can develop the agenda and produce the packet. Likewise, if you are trying to attract novices, producing a packet may help encourage participation by reducing the preparation and anxiety associated with their first tournament. On the other hand, this may serve as a disincentive if potential participants are not interested in topics that you select. Ultimately, the characteristics of your tournament's participants and the resources at your disposal should determine how to handle the agenda.

Agenda Guidelines

Use the following guidelines to help you create an agenda either from participants' suggestions or on your own:

1. **Include as much variety as possible.** Include legislation on a wide variety of topics of interest to the participants. This is especially important if you are producing your tournament's packet without soliciting the input of others. Often directors will choose topics based on their interests or their team's expertise. This can lead to an agenda that is of little interest to potential participants and works to the disadvantage of teams that may not have concentrated on those issues.

2. **Balance participation.** Make sure that you include bills and resolutions from all schools or participants. A good rule of thumb is to ask for a maximum of two bills and two resolutions from each participant or school. Use as many as possible, but remember to include a variety of topics.

3. **Fill the congress time.** Make sure that your agenda is long enough to allow debate for the full length of the time scheduled. The congress may find some pieces of legislation uninteresting and quickly move on to a different item, leaving time in the schedule. Provide two pieces of legislation per scheduled hour of deliberation plus a few extra pieces to ensure a cushion. An extra piece of legislation for every one to two hours of the session is a good rule of thumb. For example, in an 8-hour legislative day you would want to make sure your packet provides at least 20 items for deliberation.

4. **Provide the packet in a timely manner.** Distribute the legislative packet at least a week in advance of the actual congress so that participants can review and prepare.

5. **Announce whether the tournament will be open or closed.** When you distribute the agenda, indicate whether the tournament will be open to new legislation from the floor or whether your agenda is the only business that members will debate. Determining whether the tournament is open or closed depends on the type of participants you are hosting. Newer participants will probably prefer the certainty of a closed agenda; more experienced students will enjoy the competition that spontaneous debate allows.

Tabulation Materials

Make sure that you have all the materials your judges and tab staff will need to compile the results of your tournament. These include the following:

1. **Copies of the official score sheets** (see Chapter 13 for more details). You can create score sheets by using a spreadsheet program. Place competitor names in the left-hand column and number the speeches across the top row. You can then easily adjust the names during registration, if necessary. To ensure accuracy, do not make copies for judges until after registration is complete.

2. **Computer.** Make sure you have access to a computer and copies of any tabulation programs or files you will need during the tournament. You will also need a printer to print judging sheets, results, and other necessary materials.

3. **Photocopier.** If possible, make sure a photocopier is available throughout your session so that you can duplicate the tournament's results as well as packets of legislation, amendments, additional ballots, and other materials that may run short as the tournament progresses.

Participant Materials

As host, you are responsible for providing the materials the participants need during the session. You should supply each member with a copy of the legislation slated for debate, several copies of the amendment form (Appendix 8), and copies of the ballots used for voting (Appendix 10). If you are asking the participants to rank outstanding members, you must supply the appropriate ballot as well (Appendix 11). (See Chapter 13 for more information on balloting by members.) You might also want to provide additional materials—extra paper, pens, pencils—as well as Internet connections, although these are not required.

Judge/Presiding Officer Materials

You must provide the judge with the official score sheet and, if you choose to use them, sample ballots (Appendix 9) to aid in judging. The judge also needs a seating chart to keep track of who has spoken. Make sure that the chart is accurate and indicates clearly the names and seating positions of all participants.

Additionally, you should provide the presiding officer and parliamentarian with a brief guide to the rules of procedure. The tables available in Appendix 3 summarize this information for quick access. Often, disputes are prolonged because the officers cannot effectively use the rules to manage deliberations. By providing the tools to facilitate this process, you will limit these breakdowns in debate, which detract from your tournament's success.

Wellness Room

The host usually provides a wellness room for coaches, tournament staff, and competitors. This room offers participants a place to take a short break from the congress. While often overlooked, this aspect of tournament hosting can contribute greatly to your event's success. Providing light refreshments, newspapers, television, and other distractions is a helpful way to reduce the stress of everyone involved. Additionally, the wellness room provides a comfortable place for people to gather while awaiting the resolution of any problems. As your experience with hosting tournaments increases, you will learn the importance of keeping participants happy. Having a wellness room is a good way to do this.

Tab Staff

You will need a dedicated staff of three or four people to tabulate the results of your tournament. When choosing who will run the tabulation, look to the sponsors of debate activities from other schools. They are more likely to understand the process, or at least the logic behind it, than individuals with no experience, and thus will be more efficient at the task. Most important, select people who are honest and reliable. Tabulating is one of the central parts of the tournament. If your staff fails to produce the results in a timely manner or if the results are full of inaccuracies, you bear the responsibility for a lot of unhappy participants.

Other Staff

You will also need people to monitor the session, help count votes and ballots in the assembly, manage the wellness room, organize clean-up, and serve as errand runners, when necessary.

With tournaments, the old adage "an ounce of prevention beats a pound of cure" holds true. The more you think about what needs and problems may arise, and plan for them, the fewer the problems in the long term.

During the Congress

As the host, your role changes once the congress begins. If you have prepared thoroughly, you have only a limited amount of work, but the tasks are important.

1. **Check materials and facilities.** Make sure all the materials needed are in place. Also inspect the tabulation room, wellness room, and any other areas that the congress will use.

2. **Monitor registration.** Make sure that the official score sheets and seating charts remain accurate in light of any last minute dropouts, name changes, or other problems. If you have access to a laptop computer, you may want to make these changes on the spot as participants check in, and release the charts and score sheets after the registration period ends. Otherwise, you should print out the ones you created before the tournament and carefully note changes so that when you return to the computer, you can make the updates and quickly get the tournament underway. If you do not have access to a laptop, make sure you allow time in your schedule to produce and distribute the documents before the deliberations begin. If you have instituted a withdrawal deadline, you should have minimal changes. If participants drop out during the tournament, ask judges to cross out their scores on the ballot. By doing so, you should be able to produce accurate results and resolve any problems with little difficulty.

3. **Welcome the participants and start the session's business.** Typically, the host offers a few short remarks (two to three minutes) to begin the session and designates someone from the staff to conduct elections so that deliberation can begin.

After the session begins, step away and let your staff members do their jobs. Do not disturb the tabulation staff, the assistants hosting the wellness room, or those involved in other assembly functions. Many first time hosts try to control every aspect of the tournament. Unfortunately, this only undermines efficiency. Instead, move around the tournament, making sure that everything is functioning smoothly. Following the end of deliberations, make sure that the judges' ballots reach the tab room for calculation and that the participants remain patiently in a designated area to await the results.

Once the tabulation staff has compiled the results, ask the participants to reassemble in the session's chamber for the awards ceremony. (Make sure that you list the ceremony in your tournament schedule so that everyone gathers without having to be reminded.) At this point, offer any parting words, "thank yous," and trophies or certificates you are awarding the outstanding participants. In the meantime, direct your tabulation staff to copy the results for each participant or participant's school for immediate distribution. The sooner the participants can see the details, the sooner you will be able to stop explaining the results.

After the Tournament

Often new hosts mistakenly believe that their work is over once the participants leave. However, you still have a few important tasks to perform. Immediately after the session ends, you must supervise the clean-up. You also have to resolve any tabulation disputes that may arise and make sure that you retain copies of the records so that they are available to participants, if needed. And remember to thank your staff and volunteers!

Contact local media with the results and highlights of the congress. Community newspapers, local radio, and other media outlets are often interested in giving coverage to local youth organizations. Gaining attention from the community is an invaluable way to generate more support for your program. Community members are often more willing to support your efforts once they know more about your competitions.

Finally, remember to solicit feedback from participants. Their responses are important in helping you improve future events.

Once you have completed these tasks, you have fulfilled your responsibilities. As you may have surmised, the key to hosting a successful student congress is in the work you do before the tournament begins. With the right preparation, the tournament will run smoothly; without adequate preparation it will likely be disastrous. Following the guidelines in this chapter, allowing yourself ample time, and relying on a trustworthy staff should put you on your way to managing a competitive student congress that is enjoyable for everyone.

KEY CONCEPTS FROM CHAPTER 12

Prior to the Tournament

- Make provisions for necessary space.
- Set a date.
- Gather materials for tabulation.
- Gather materials for assembly members, presiding officer, and judges.
- Make plans for a wellness room.
- Choose a tabulation staff.
- Create a legislation packet.
- Generate an invitation.

During the Tournament

- Double-check materials.
- Monitor registration.
- Welcome participants and begin the session.
- Conduct awards assembly.
- Ensure participants are provided copies of results.

After the Tournament

- Gather feedback.
- Pursue media coverage.

Chapter 13
Tabulation: Evaluating the Competitors*

Tabulation, or "tabbing," is the process by which the judge's evaluation of the competitors is recorded, tallied, and compared to the other participants to determine the best assembly members. It is one of the most important aspects of sponsoring a competitive student congress and one that demands extreme care in processing large amounts of data. This chapter introduces the popular methods of tabulating, discusses the considerations involved in choosing a method, describes how to use these techniques, and offers some guidelines for running the tab room. Tabbing can be complicated. However, with a little preparation and thoroughly trained judges, it can run as seamlessly as the session itself.[1]

Tabulation Staff
The tabulation staff is responsible for three tasks: preparing the tabulation system and materials, collecting and computing the results, and determining the superior participants. In addition, the staff offers verification of the results to competitors and coaches. The tabulation staff has very little interaction with the actual session. Instead, staff members work in a tab room, where judges report their scores at the end of the session.

Tabulation Methods
Tournaments traditionally use one of two tab methods. The first is simple and the more traditional of the two. Referred to as the "priority system," it adds the number of points awarded to each participant. The other system, developed by the National Forensic League, is used in most competitive

---

*Kari E. Wohlschlegel and Michael K. Middleton

congress sessions in the United States. Known as the "base system," it attempts to make ranking more equitable by creating a common denominator based on the possible number of speeches given in the session.

CONSIDERATIONS WHEN SELECTING A TABULATION METHOD

Remember that there is no "right" method of tabbing. You can choose your method based on your experience, level of comfort, or even personal preference, but you must inform the judges and participants which method you will use before the congress begins. The system you choose will impact what type of competition your tournament rewards, so in selecting a method, consider three factors: size, tournament goals, and resources.

Size

How large is your congress? In a small assembly with only a few participants vying for speaking time, all members will have an equal opportunity to speak and so to be evaluated. In this case, you may choose to use the simpler priority system. On the other hand, if you are hosting a sizable session, perhaps one involving multiple schools or a league competition, you may want to use the base system, which accounts for disparities in speaking opportunities that sometimes arise in very large assemblies.

Tournament Goals

What do you want to reward? Are there pedagogical goals you wish to fulfill? Or is there a certain type of excellence in participation that you wish to reward? In other words, why have you decided to host the congress?

If you are trying to generate interest in the event among new competitors, you may want to use the priority system, which rewards the quantity of participation. Knowing that each speech will be judged independently and that doing poorly on one does not necessarily mean that one's hopes are sunk is often encouraging to novice competitors.

Alternately, if you are hosting an event for more experienced competitors, you may want to use the base system, which rewards the quality as well as the number of speeches. This system permits members who give a smaller number of excellent speeches to receive higher rankings than those who give a larger number of poor-to-average speeches.

Resources

What resources do you have for tabulation? How many people do you have to help you with your tabulation? What sort of computer access do you have? Are you on a tight schedule or are there breaks in the session—workshops, meals, or other down time—that give you an opportunity to enter scores up to that point and, thus, expedite the final tabulation at the tournament's end? The answers to these questions will help determine which tabulation system you use. Obviously, the priority system is the easier method. If you have limited resources, you may be safest choosing this system. You might also want to consider this system if you have no experience with tabulation. Much like the competitors you host, a bad first experience may sour you on this type of tournament because you chose a method of tabulation that is too complicated based on the experience of you and your staff. However, the base system is not without its own merits. If you are lucky enough to have all the resources you need, the base system allows an increased focus on the quality, not quantity, of participation.

Finally, the league in which you compete may also determine the system you use. For example, the National Forensic League requires its National Student Congress Competition to use the base system to ensure that inequitable speaking opportunities do not impact the results.

TABULATION SYSTEMS

The Priority System

The priority system is the simpler of the tabulation methods and requires little explanation or experience to use effectively. The first step in the priority system is to determine the maximum number of speeches that a participant may give in a session. You should decide this prior to the tournament and include this information in the invitation or with the materials you distribute when participants arrive at the assembly. In student congresses in the United States, this number is usually five.

You must also decide what to do if all members have given the maximum number of speeches and time still remains in the assembly. In a large session, this will probably not be a problem, but in smaller sessions, classroom competitions, and intramural sessions, you must have a procedure for managing such occurrences. In these instances, you may allow participants to give additional speeches without receiving more points. Alternately, you may allow additional speeches and permit the competitors to substitute the score from one of these speeches for one of the first five. If you allow substitution, make sure that no participant has more than five speeches included for official tabulation.

When using the priority system, you must follow the principle that members who have spoken little or not at all speak first. Thus, this method of tabulation requires judges, parliamentarians, and presiding officers to ensure that all participants who wish to speak have given their first speech before members give their second, and so on.

Prior to the opening of the session, you must supply the judge with an official score sheet that includes the names of all participants and space to enter scores for each of their five speeches, as well as space for more scores if you are permitting additional speeches. Because judges use this sheet to report scores back to the tabulation staff, you should create only one copy per judge to avoid errors or mistakes when the scores are authenticated and computed. You also need to prepare a seating chart to help judges, as well as the presiding officer and parliamentarian, identify which participant is speaking. Below is an example of a completed score sheet.

After you have completed these steps, the session can begin. As the tournament progresses, the judges enter scores for each of the participants' speeches, and at the end of the session, return the official score sheet to the tabulation center. Once the tab staff receives these sheets, the tabulation process begins.

First, the staff reviews the data to determine its accuracy and legibility. Make sure that the judges remain until you have completed this step so that they can clarify any issues. Next, the tab staff verifies the data; if additional speeches can be substituted, as described above, it drops the lowest scores. The staff then generates total points for each participant, lists the participants in rank order, and identifies the top five point earners. You can break a tie by determining the best average score of the tied participants. You can also drop the highest and lowest scores and sum up or average the remaining scores, or both, if necessary.

Recognizing Superior Performance
You may use the top five list to recognize the superior participants or you may involve assembly members by asking them to rank the final five.

Official Score Sheet

Speech / Contestant Name	1	2	3	4	5	6	7	8	9	10	11	Total (Tab Only)
						For additional speeches, consult tournament rules on scoring.						
Doe, J.	4	5	3	6	3							21
Smith, C.	2	3	4	5	4							19
Jones, A.	4	4	5	2								15
Bro0wn, J.	2	2										4
Russell, N.	6	6	6	2	3							23

NOTE: In this model, only the first five speeches have been scored. Some tournaments may score more, drop high or low scores, etc.

Regardless of the system you choose, you must announce it prior to the tournament.

If you wish the assembly members to take part in the final selection process, place the names of the top five competitors randomly on a ballot and submit it to the full session for a vote. The members then rank their choices from 1 to 5, with 1 their first choice. Tabulation officials use the steps below to determine the *majority* of the assembly's first, second, third, etc., choices.

First Counting

To tabulate the final ballots, begin by arranging them in separate piles based on who receives a first-place vote. Once this is completed, record the number of first-place votes each person receives. For example, in an assembly with 10 members you would receive 10 ballots for the top five spots (Adams, Brown, Cole, Davis, Evans). The ballots might look as follows.

Ballot 1	Ballot 2	Ballot 3	Ballot 4	Ballot 5
1. Adams	1. Adams	1. Brown	1. Adams	1. Davis
2. Brown	2. Cole	2. Cole	2. Brown	2. Adams
3. Cole	3. Brown	3. Evans	3. Cole	3. Brown
4. Davis	4. Davis	4. Davis	4. Davis	4. Cole
5. Evans	5. Evans	5. Adams	5. Evans	5. Evans

Ballot 6	Ballot 7	Ballot 8	Ballot 9	Ballot 10
1. Adams	1. Brown	1. Brown	1. Davis	1. Cole
2. Brown	2. Evans	2. Davis	2. Adams	2. Brown
3. Cole	3. Davis	3. Evans	3. Brown	3. Adams
4. Davis	4. Adams	4. Cole	4. Cole	4. Davis
5. Evans	5. Cole	5. Adams	5. Evans	5. Evans

After sorting by first-place votes, the results would be

Adams' pile: 4 ballots

Brown's pile: 3 ballots

Cole's pile: 1 ballot

Davis' pile: 2 ballots

Evans: Since Evans received no first-place votes, he falls out of consideration in the preferential balloting.

Second Counting

Next, select the pile of ballots with the fewest first-place votes (in this case Cole's) and redistribute to the pile of the person ranked second place on these ballots. In this case, Ballot 10 voted Cole 1 and Brown 2, so Brown would receive Ballot 10's vote for first place. Physically move the ballots from the stack with the fewest first-place votes to the stacks of their second place choice and place these ballots at the bottom of the appropriate pile or piles. In our example, you would physically put Ballot 10 at the bottom of Brown's pile. Then, recount the remaining ballots. Using the example above, the resulting piles would include the following ballot counts:

Adams: 4 ballots

Brown: 4 ballots (the original three plus Cole's)

Davis: 2 ballots

Subsequent Countings

Repeat the process with the next smallest pile of ballots until a single member has a majority of the votes for first place. If we return to our example, no one has a majority of the ballots, and Davis has the next smallest pile. Therefore, Ballots 5 and 9, which list Davis in first place, would be distributed to Adams since Adams is listed second on both ballots. The resulting piles would include the following counts:

Adams: 6 ballots (the original four plus two from Davis)

Brown: 4 ballots

At this point Adams has a majority. The tab staff then crosses out the first-place vote on each ballot and repeats the process to determine second, third, fourth, and fifth places. The staff releases the results to the tournament director and the awards ceremony begins.

The Base System

Preparation for using the base system is similar to that for using the priority system. When you issue your invitation, you must inform all tournament participants and officials that you will be scoring on the base system and that there is no limit to the number of speeches.

The day of the tournament, your tabulation staff must determine the exact number of participants. This is important for determining the "base." The tab staff then provides officials a score sheet listing the name of the participants with spaces for points next to each. Unlike the score sheet used in the priority system, the base score sheet does not include spaces for a predetermined maximum number of speeches. Instead, it includes a larger number of spaces next to each name, since the total number of speeches is unknown. Because speakers may give as many speeches as they wish, the judge, parliamentarian, and especially the presiding officer must ensure that no one speaks twice before every other member has spoken or has had the opportunity to speak for the first time.

As with the priority system, the judges return their score sheets, and the tabulation staff makes sure it has no questions before the judges leave. Then the staff begins the process that distinguishes the base system.

The base system works by determining how many times all members of the session have had the opportunity to speak. That number is the base the assembly has reached. For example, a tournament begins on base one. Once everyone has had an opportunity to speak, the assembly moves to base two. Once every member has had the chance to speak twice, the assembly advances to base three. The tab staff can determine what base the assembly has reached by referring to the base calculation table provided in Appendix 14 or in the NFL Online Student Congress Manual. For example, a 20-member assembly has reached base 2 after 22 speeches; base 3 after 42; and so on. Some tournaments announce when the assembly has reached a new base. If you choose to do so, assign a tab staff member to monitor the assembly and make the announcement, or remind the judge to do so.

Once the tab staff determines the base, they must determine the number of speeches each member has given and the total number of points awarded each member. They then divide the member's total points by his or her number of speeches to calculate the average number of points earned per speech. This is called the raw average. Once the staff has calculated all the raw averages, they multiply these numbers by the base. For example, if the assembly reaches base 2, every member's raw average is multiplied by 2. The equation is as follows:

$$\frac{\text{total number of points}}{\text{total number of speeches}} \quad \text{x} \quad 2$$

The following example illustrates how the base system works. The assembly has reached base 2, and the competitors have earned the following points:

Official Score Sheet

Contestant	Speech 1	Speech 2	Speech 3	Total Points	Number of Speeches	Contestant Averages	Contestant's Final Score avg. x base
Bill	2	2	2	6	3	2	4
Sally	4	5		9	2	4.5	9
Jill	2	3		5	2	2.5	5

Once the staff produces these scores, they rank them, with ties broken to the 4th decimal point. They then place the top five competitors on a ballot and conduct the preferential balloting procedure described above to generate the final rankings.

The base method ensures that participants are not penalized merely because they did not give the same number of speeches as their peers. It allows the members who gave the better overall speeches to receive higher honors than the speakers who gave the most speeches. It shifts the focus from quantity of speeches to quality of performance and thus increases the competitive rigor of a tournament.

Suggestions for Successful Tabulation

1. **When possible, use multiple judges.** Often, more judges mean a better result. Averaging multiple scores for each speech before performing the base or priority tabbing operations mitigates the impact of unusually generous or rigorous judging.

2. **Be open to participants.** An inexperienced tab staff will often close the tab room to everyone but their assistants. While this minimizes distractions and helps avoid mistakes, coaches and participants become suspicious of tab rooms that are too secretive and unwilling to share information. You need to maintain a balance. As a general rule, more access to more information increases the learning experience and often the satisfaction of tournament participants.

3. **Stay focused on the task at hand.** While you want to be open to inquiries from tournament participants, you must balance this with your primary task—producing accurate results. Little is more heartbreaking for new competitors than to find that their successes or failures were not accurately measured because of simple mathematical errors. The best tab room staff will make a minor mistake at one point or another, but you can help minimize this by keeping visitors out of the tab room when you are calculating the results. Explain that you want to minimize distractions to ensure accurate results and remind your visitors that the information they need will be available and verifiable shortly.

4. **Double-check your work.** Mistakes can happen easily. You may misread a column, press a wrong calculator button, or forget to save a spreadsheet file. When tabbing, two heads really are better than one. Every tabulation staff should have at least two members: one to calculate results and another to verify those calculations. It is far better to catch mistakes in the tab room than in front of an entire awards assembly, when it's both troublesome to make a correction and will

likely upset both the student who benefits and the one who may be negatively impacted by the calculation error.

5. **Use a computer.** Using a computer helps minimize tabulation errors. You can carry out much of the repetitive math—that invites slight mistakes but has massive consequences—with the click of a mouse. If you have access to a computer and basic spreadsheet software, you may find that entering the tournament roster and simple mathematical spreadsheet formulas significantly increases the speed of your final tabulation. Additionally, this approach allows you to efficiently provide participants their own copies of the results in an understandable form.

6. **Make copies of score sheets and tabbing sheets.** As you have learned, being open with participants, coaches, and sponsors helps ensure a successful tournament. Consequently, make copies of all the tabulation materials your congress produces. This includes score sheets, spreadsheets, and results lists. Any documentation that shows how you reached your results will allow participants to verify their placement in the tournament or to point out a mistake you can avoid in the future.

7. **Be adaptable.** Adaptability is key for a successful tab staff. You may encounter unforeseen problems even in the most carefully planned tournament—a computer may malfunction, forcing you to tab by hand, or a judge may disappear before you can verify a score. However, remaining adaptable will prevent these problems from turning into disasters that ruin your tournament and the competitors' experience. By following the steps in this chapter and remaining patient and adaptable, you should have a successful tournament.

Tabulation Defined

- Tabulation, or "tabbing," is the process of calculating the tournament's results to determine whose performances will be awarded as superior.

Considerations When Choosing a Tabbing Method

- Your experience level
- Size of tournament
- What you want to recognize in your competition
- Available resources

Tabulation Systems

- The priority system is simple and rewards quantity of speeches. It is less taxing on new or small tabulation staffs.
- The base system, used by the National Forensic League in U.S. competitions, is a more complex system that emphasizes the quality of speeches.

Suggestions for Successful Tabulation

- Use multiple judges.
- Be open to participants.
- Stay focused on task at hand.
- Double-check your work.
- Use a computer, when possible.
- Photocopy all records.
- Be flexible.

NOTE

1. The tabulation and tournament administration methods in this book are based on the National Forensic League (NFL) Rules for Student Congress. However, they are not the official interpretation of these rules. The final arbiter of questions about rules and procedure for NFL sanctioned events is the NFL Student Congress Manual and other official NFL documents available on its Web site. Nonetheless, we hope this book helps clarify many of the issues that confront both novice and seasoned competitors and coaches.

Appendixes

Appendix 1:
Seven Ways to Encourage Engagement and Quality Debate

Debating topics of interest to the participants is the main goal of student congresses. Occasionally, debates may drag or become entangled in parliamentary procedure. Below are suggestions for encouraging quality debate and moving the agenda along.

1. *Encourage Members to Prepare Resolutions and Bills before the Session*
   By gathering resolutions and bills and distributing them as a legislative agenda before the session, you enable participants to research the resolution topics so that they can conduct a well-informed debate.

3. *Announce a Theme for the Session*
   This strategy allows members to narrow their research and come to the session better prepared. It also helps limit the range of topics the resolutions and bills might address and thus focuses the debate.

4. *Encourage the Use of Amendments*
   Encouraging the use of amendments promotes critical thinking about civic issues, one of the goals of student congresses. Amendments can lead to spirited debate and improve the motions before the house. Often, sessions will debate a main motion, take a vote, and move on. While this is sometimes appropriate in the case of exceptionally well thought-out motions, more often members can better each other's work by scrutinizing it and suggesting changes.

5. *Use Committees*
   Committees are an especially useful way for members to work through the ideas and issues related to main motions. The informal atmosphere

of a small group often encourages spirited and challenging debate. Members feel more comfortable than they do in the larger assembly, where proceedings are more formal and where they have to vie with a large number of participants for the opportunity to speak.

6. *Move through the Voting Process Quickly*

   The voting process can often be one of the most time-consuming parts of a student congress. Because it takes time away from the assembly's main goal-debating issues, you should move it along as expeditiously as possible. Use general consent whenever possible and consider developing a consent agenda to consolidate routine business and dispose of it at one time, rather than having the assembly vote on each element separately.

7. *Make Sure the Chair Knows How to Expedite Business and Encourage Debate*

   The chair can be invaluable in keeping debate flowing. Make sure the chair knows the importance of the following:

   a. <u>Understanding the rules of procedure</u>. Arguing about rules or even consulting the parliamentarian takes time. If the chair has a clear understanding of the assembly's rules, she will be able to move debate along.

   b. <u>Keeping the focus on motions</u>. If a member attempts to deliver a speech rather than offer or address a motion, the chair should politely phrase the speaker's theme as a motion and ask if that is what the member intends. If a member begins discussing a tangential or different subject, the chair should remind that member of the motion on the floor.

   c. <u>Dealing quickly with dilatory motions</u>. The chair should rule them out of order or refuse to recognize members who use these tactics.

Appendix 2
Secondary Motions

The chart on the following pages presents an overview of how to handle secondary motions. We list the subsidiary, privileged, and incidental motions in rank order. Subsidiary motions yield to privileged, which yield to incidental. The motions at the top of each chart yield to those below it. Note: unclassified motions have no rank.

Subsidiary Motions

Motion	Purpose	Second Required
Postpone Indefinitely	avoid a motion	yes
Amend	make changes	yes
Commit/Refer	create a committee	yes
Postpone Definitely	set debate for later time	yes
Limit/Extend Debate	limit consideration	yes
Previous Question	close debate; force vote	yes
Lay on the Table	postpone and consider other business	yes

Debatable	Amendable	Required Vote	May Interrupt a Speaker
yes	no	majority	no
yes	no	majority	no
yes	yes	majority	no
yes	yes	majority	no
no	yes	majority	no
no	no	two-thirds	no
no	no	two-thirds	no

Privileged Motions

Motion	Purpose	Second Required
Call for the Orders of the Day	enforce agenda	no
Raise a Question of Privilege	attend to special needs	no
Recess	short break	yes
Adjourn	close and end debate	yes
Fix Time to Which to Adjourn	end assembly; set next meeting	yes

Debatable	Amendable	Required Vote	May interrupt a speaker
no	no	chair's decision	yes, if necessary
no	no	chair's decision	yes, rarely
no	yes; time	majority	no
no	no	majority	no
no	no	majority	no

Incidental Motions

Motion	Purpose	Second Required
Point of Order	call for proper procedure	no
Appeal	dispute chair's ruling	yes
Suspend the Rules	relax procedure	yes
Division of Assembly	standing vote	no
Request and Inquiries		
1. Parliamentary inquiry	solicit chair's advice on rules	no
2. Point of information	question a speaker	no
3. Requests to withdraw a motion	remove a motion from debate	yes
4. Request for any other privilege	special uses	yes

Debatable	Amendable	Required Vote	May Interrupt a Speaker
no	no	chair's decision	yes
yes	no	majority	yes
no	no	two-thirds	no
no	no	automatic	no
no	no	no	yes
no	no	no	yes
no	no	majority	yes
no	no	majority, request based	yes

Unclassified Motions		
Motion	**Purpose**	**Second Required**
Take from the Table	bring back before assembly a motion laid on table	yes
Rescind or Amend Something Previously Adopted	adjust text of an adopted motion	yes
Discharge a Committee	remove question from further committee consideration and bring it to full assembly	yes

Debatable	Amendable	Required Vote	May Interrupt a Speaker
no	no	majority	no
yes	yes	two-thirds	no
yes	yes	majority	no

Appendix 3

Proper Form for Making and Dispensing with Motions

Member's Example	Chair's Example
Main Motion "I move to consider [state declaration/motion]." "I second." (This is the proper form when a second is necessary.)	**Main Motion** "It has been moved and seconded; the motion under consideration is [state description]."
Postpone Indefinitely "I move the resolution be postponed indefinitely."	**Postpone Indefinitely** "It has been moved and seconded; the house will now consider postponement."
Amend "I move to amend by adding/ deleting/replacing [explain change]."	**Amend** "The assembly will now consider the amendment that [state change under debate]."
Commit/Refer to Committee "I move the motion be referred to a committee of [fill in specifics] appointed by [fill in specifics]."	**Commit/Refer to Committee** "It has been moved to refer to committee; the house will consider the referral." *(continues)*

Postpone to a Certain Time (or Definitely)

"I move to postpone the question to the next meeting [or some other time]."

Postpone to a Certain Time (or Definitely)

"The motion before the assembly is to postpone until [time]; the house will now consider postponement."

Limit or Extend Limits of Debate

"I move that debate be limited to five-minute speeches [or some other time]."

Limit or Extend Limits of Debate

"It has been moved that debate be limited or extended on the motion; the house will now consider limits."

Previous Question

"I move the previous question."

Previous Question

"The previous question has been moved; the house will consider the motion for previous question." (If approved, the motion this applied to will be voted on.)

Lay on the Table

"I move the motion be laid on the table."

Lay on the Table

"The motion is to table the bill; the house will now consider tabling the motion [state specific motion]."

Call for the Orders of the Day

"I call for the orders of the day."

Call for the Orders of the Day

"The orders have been called; the assembly will now consider [state proper business]."

(*continues*)

Appendix 3 (*continued*)

Raise a Question of Privilege	**Raise a Question of Privilege**
"I rise to a question of privilege."	(This motion is solved by a chair's decision on how to handle the special request.)
Recess	**Recess**
"I move to recess for five [or any number of] minutes."	"A recess has been moved; the house will now consider the recess."

Source: Henry M. Robert III, William J. Evans, Daniel H. Honemann, and Thomas J. Balch, eds., "Charts, Tables and Lists," in *Robert's Rules of Order*, Newly Revised, 10th ed. (Cambridge, Mass.: Perseus Publishing, 2000), pp. 30-42.

Appendix 4
Sample Minutes

Assembly Name:

Date:

Chair:

Minutes keeper:

Minutes:

> *Main Motion:* (insert title of motion made)
> Description of information, e.g., vote, names of speaking members, name of member who originated the motion, etc.
>
> > Secondary Motion: (insert title of motion made)
> > Description of information, e.g., vote, names of speaking members, name of member who originated the motion, etc.
> >
> > Secondary Motion: (continue process until no business is pending and another main motion is made).
>
> *Main Motion:* (insert title of motion made)
>
> *One-Minute Speeches:* (insert time allotted here)
> List members who participated in speeches and topic.

Note: You may also want to include copies of the agenda, amendments, bills, resolutions, information about the election of the chair, for example, vote count, nominations, roll in attendance, etc., in the minutes.

Appendix 5
Sample Student Congress Schedule

Sample Session Schedule	
9:00 am	Registration (9–9:30) Establish Seating Chart or Roll of Participants in Attendance Take Nominations for Chair Elect Chair Call to Order Adopt Agenda
10:00 am –1:00 pm	Regular Business Begins Floor is open to motions* Members may introduce bills, resolutions, etc., as motions during this time
1–2:00 pm	Midday Recess
2–5:00 pm	Regular Business Continues
4–5:00 pm	*If necessary, this time in the regular schedule can be set aside to take up postponed or committee-referred motions*
5:00 pm	Adjournment of the Assembly

*Whether motions come from an agenda or from the members on the floor depends on the nature of the agenda adopted. The agenda is only the initially prescribed order.

Appendix 6
Resolution Template

(TITLE OF RESOLUTION*)

Submitted By: (Your name [and, if applicable, your supporters' names])

Date:

Whereas (insert observations about the causes and effects of the problem your resolution addresses);

And, Whereas (if more premises are necessary to describe the problem, continue adding them; if not, the next set of clauses should explain the scope of the problem);

And, Whereas (after completing the clauses describing the problem and its scope, the next set of clauses should be those outlining reasons the resolution should be acted on);

Therefore, Be It Resolved, by the Student Congress here assembled, that (include the position or action the assembly should take)

Insomuch as we believe this action should be to the benefit of our community, the present resolution offers the following benefits:**

First, (include the first benefit the action or position offers).

Second, (include second benefit).

Third, (include third benefit).

---

* The title should reflect the issue the resolution addresses.

** The benefits portion is necessary only when you believe your resolution needs further justification.

Appendix 7
Bill Template

(TITLE)

Be it enacted by Student Congress here assembled, that:

Section 1. (*Here you identify the specific policy your bill would enact if passed by the congress.*)

Section 2. (*You next identify any exceptions to its enforcement or other nuances of its enactment.*)

Section 3. (*Finally, you include the enforcement clause in which you articulate what the consequences of non-compliance will be.*)

Appendix 8
Amendment Form

Title: _____ .

Submitted by:

Date:

Original text, or identify where addition or subtraction is to be made:
_____
_____
_____
_____
_____

New text: _____
_____
_____
_____
_____

Type of change: _____
_____

For Chair's use:

Accepted: (   )   Rejected: (   )

Appendix 9

Optional Student Congress Ballot*

Verbal Elements

Fluency—Does the speaker stumble on their words excessively?

Poor 1   2   3   4   5   6 Excellent

Vocal Variety—Is the speaker monotone or do they use their voice effectively?

Poor 1   2   3   4   5   6 Excellent

Clear Imagery—Does the speaker make the issue clearly understandable, i.e., does the speaker "paint a picture" for the audience?

Poor 1   2   3   4   5   6 Excellent

Word Choice—Does the speaker use effective word choices, rhetorical devices, etc.?

Poor 1   2   3   4   5   6 Excellent

Humor—Does the speaker attempt to use humor? Is it in good taste?

Poor 1   2   3   4   5   6 Excellent

Effective Language—Does the speaker use active, forceful, direct language or is he or she ambiguous, passive, timid?

Poor 1   2   3   4   5   6 Excellent

Appropriateness—Does the speaker attack any group or person? Does the speaker foster an open environment?

Poor 1   2   3   4   5   6 Excellent

Nonverbal Elements

Use of Notes—Does the speaker use notes in a limited fashion?

Poor 1   2   3   4   5   6 Excellent

Eye Contact—Does the speaker use effective eye contact with the entire audience?

Poor 1   2   3   4   5   6 Excellent

Gestures—Does the speaker use effective gestures or distracting ones?

Poor 1   2   3   4   5   6 Excellent

Posture & Demeanor—Is the speaker confident, forceful, inviting?

Poor 1   2   3   4   5   6 Excellent

Argument Elements

Organization—Does the speech "make sense" as you listen to it?

Poor 1   2   3   4   5   6 Excellent

Relevance—Are the arguments relevant to the direction in which the debate is moving?

Poor 1   2   3   4   5   6 Excellent

Responsive—Does it address the topics under discussion directly?

Poor 1   2   3   4   5   6 Excellent

Internally Sound—Are assertions properly supported?

Poor 1   2   3   4   5   6 Excellent

Use of Evidence—Does the speaker responsibly use quality evidence?

Poor 1   2   3   4   5   6 Excellent

Argument Elements (*continued*)					
Sound Logic—Does the speaker rely on spurious relationships to warrant claims?					
Poor 1	2	3	4	5	6 Excellent
Quality of Implications—Does the speaker answer the "so what?" question?					
Poor 1	2	3	4	5	6 Excellent
TOTAL SCORE:					

*Use this ballot as a guide or fill it out and average the individual scores to determine an individual's average on a speech.

Appendix 10
Legislative Ballot

Legislative Ballot

(Sample)

Resolution Title: _____

Your Name: _____

Circle One:

          Yea   Nay   Abstain

Appendix 11
Preferential Ballot

Preferential Ballot
(Sample)

Please list your choice of candidates in order of preference:

1.

2.

3.

4.

5.

Appendix 12
Official Score Sheet: Priority System

Official Score Sheet Priority System

Speech	1	2	3	4	5	6	7	8	9	10	11	Total (Tab Only)
Contestant Name												

For additional speeches, consult tournament rules on scoring.

Appendix 13
Official Score Sheet: Base System

Official Score Sheet: Base System

Contestant Name	Speech	1	2	3	4	5	6	7	8	9	10	Total (Tab Use Only)

Appendix 14
Base Calculation Table

Base Calculation Table*										
Participants in session	**Base Completed**									
	1	2	3	4	5	6	7	8	9	10
10	12	22	32	42	52	62	72	82	92	102
11	13	24	35	46	57	68	79	90	101	112
12	14	26	38	50	62	74	86	98	110	122
13	15	28	41	54	67	80	93	106	119	132
14	16	30	44	58	72	86	100	114	128	142
15	17	32	47	62	77	92	107	122	137	152
20	22	42	62	82	102	122	142	162	182	202
25	27	52	77	102	127	152	177	202	227	252
30	32	62	92	122	152	182	212	242	272	302
35	37	72	107	142	177	212	247	282	317	352

*The numbers in the left column are the number of participants in the session. The numbers along the top row represent bases completed. At the intersection of these two numbers is the total number of speeches that must be given for a base to be completed. For example, after 22 speeches a base 1 assembly of 10 members will become a base 2 assembly. To determine the base for numbers not on the chart, begin by calculating base 1. You do this by adding 2 to the number of participants. For example, with 26 participants base 1 equals 28. For each additional base, add the number of members in the assembly to the number you calculated as base 1, e.g., with 26 participants base two equals 54, or 28 plus 26. You may also refer to the NFL's Student Congress Manual for a more detailed table. Remember to check regularly, as this text is revised and updated on a consistent basis. (This chart is based on chart in the NFL's Student Congress Manual, available at http://www.nflonline.org/uploads/DistrictInformation/conman.pdf.)